EYE ON
Art

# LEONARDO DA VINCI

by Don Nardo

**LUCENT BOOKS**
*A part of Gale, Cengage Learning*

GALE
CENGAGE Learning·

Detroit • New York • San Francisco • New Haven, Conn • Waterville, Maine • London

**LIBRARY OF CONGRESS CATALOGING-IN-PUBLICATION DATA**

Nardo, Don, 1947-
  Leonardo da Vinci / by Don Nardo.
    p. cm. -- (Eye on art)
  Includes bibliographical references and index.
  ISBN 978-1-4205-0735-5 (hardcover)
  1. Leonardo, da Vinci, 1452-1519--Juvenile literature. 2. Artists--Italy--Biography--Juvenile literature. 3. Art, Renaissance--Italy--Juvenile literature. I. Leonardo, da Vinci, 1452-1519. II. Title.
  N6923.L33N37 2012
  709.2--dc23
  [B]
                                                        2011042978

Lucent Books
27500 Drake Rd
Farmington Hills MI 48331

ISBN-13: 978-1-4205-0735-5
ISBN-10: 1-4205-0735-4

Printed in the United States of America
1 2 3 4 5 6 7 16 15 14 13 12

# CONTENTS

# Foreword

Some thirty-one thousand years ago, early humans painted strikingly sophisticated images of horses, bison, rhinoceroses, bears, and other animals on the walls of a cave in southern France. The meaning of these elaborate pictures is unknown, although some experts speculate that they held ceremonial significance. Regardless of their intended purpose, the Chauvet-Pont-d'Arc cave paintings represent some of the first known expressions of the artistic impulse.

From the Paleolithic era to the present day, human beings have continued to create works of visual art. Artists have developed painting, drawing, sculpture, engraving, and many other techniques to produce visual representations of landscapes, the human form, religious and historical events, and countless other subjects. The artistic impulse also finds expression in glass, jewelry, and new forms inspired by new technology. Indeed, judging by humanity's prolific artistic output throughout history, one must conclude that the compulsion to produce art is an inherent aspect of being human, and the results are among humanity's greatest cultural achievements: masterpieces such as the architectural marvels of ancient Greece, Michelangelo's perfectly rendered statue *David*, Vincent van Gogh's visionary painting *Starry Night*, and endless other treasures.

The creative impulse serves many purposes for society. At its most basic level, art is a form of entertainment or the means for a satisfying or pleasant aesthetic experience. But art's true power lies not in its potential to entertain and delight but in its ability to enlighten, to reveal the truth, and by doing so to uplift the human spirit and transform the human race.

One of the primary functions of art has been to serve religion. For most of Western history, for example, artists were paid by the church to produce works with religious themes and subjects. Art was thus a tool to help human beings transcend mundane, secular reality and achieve spiritual enlightenment. One of the best-known, and largest-scale, examples of Christian religious art is the Sistine Chapel in the Vatican in Rome. In 1508 Pope Julius II commissioned Italian Renaissance artist Michelangelo to paint the chapel's vaulted ceiling, an area of 640 square yards (535 sq. m). Michelangelo spent four years on scaffolding, his neck craned, creating a panoramic fresco of some three hundred human figures. His paintings depict Old Testament prophets and heroes, sibyls of Greek mythology, and nine scenes from the Book of Genesis, including the Creation of Adam, the Fall of Adam and Eve from the Garden of Eden, and the Flood. The ceiling of the Sistine Chapel is considered one of the greatest works of Western art and has inspired the awe of countless Christian pilgrims and other religious seekers. As eighteenth-century German poet and author Johann Wolfgang von Goethe wrote, "Until you have seen this Sistine Chapel, you can have no adequate conception of what man is capable of."

In addition to inspiring religious fervor, art can serve as a force for social change. Artists are among the visionaries of any culture. As such, they often perceive injustice and wrongdoing and confront others by reflecting what they see in their work. One classic example of art as social commentary was created in May 1937, during the brutal Spanish civil war. On May 1 Spanish artist Pablo Picasso learned of the recent attack on the small Basque village of Guernica by German airplanes allied with fascist forces led by Francisco Franco. The German pilots had used the village for target practice, a three-hour bombing that killed sixteen hundred civilians. Picasso, living in Paris, channeled his outrage over the massacre into his painting *Guernica*, a black, white, and gray mural that depicts dismembered animals and fractured human figures whose faces are contorted in agonized expressions. Initially, critics and the public condemned the painting as an incoherent hodgepodge, but the work soon came to be seen as a powerful antiwar statement and remains an iconic symbol of the violence and terror that dominated world events during the remainder of the twentieth century.

The impulse to create art—whether painting animals with crude pigments on a cave wall, sculpting a human form from marble, or commemorating human tragedy in a mural—thus serves many purposes. It offers an entertaining diversion, nourishes the imagination and the spirit, decorates and beautifies the world, and chronicles the age. But underlying all these functions is the desire to reveal that which is obscure—to illuminate, clarify, and perhaps ennoble. As Picasso himself stated, "The purpose of art is washing the dust of daily life off our souls."

The Eye on Art series is intended to assist readers in understanding the various roles of art in society. Each volume offers an in-depth exploration of a major artistic movement, medium, figure, or profession. All books in the series are beautifully illustrated with full-color photographs and diagrams. Riveting narrative, clear technical explanation, informative sidebars, fully documented quotes, a bibliography, and a thorough index all provide excellent starting points for research and discussion. With these features, the Eye on Art series is a useful introduction to the world of art—a world that can offer both insight and inspiration.

# Introduction

## The Universal Man

Shortly before his death in 1983, the popular historian and biographer Robert Payne movingly described "a man born in an obscure hamlet in Italy." That man "had no formal education" and "no natural advantages except a formidable intelligence." Payne continued, "Living at a time of incessant wars and at the mercy of many tyrants, [the man] opened up vast areas of human knowledge and painted so superbly that for many people he represents the single 'universal genius,' the prototype [model] of Western man in his utmost accomplishment, [a] Renaissance man in his utmost splendor."[1]

The man Payne described so eloquently was Leonardo da Vinci, an Italian artist, inventor, and scholar whose long life began in the mid-1400s and ended in the second decade of the 1500s. The use of the term *Renaissance man* to depict Leonardo was fitting. The Renaissance was the great cultural and artistic outburst that began in Italy in the mid-1300s and later spread across most of the rest of Europe. Talented people of the period were inspired by the ongoing rediscovery of the artistic, philosophic, and other legacies of Greco-Roman civilization, which had collapsed in the fifth to sixth centuries. During the Renaissance, European writers, painters, sculptors, architects, city planners, and others produced a veritable explosion of brilliant achievements.

Amidst this immense cultural output, a number of individuals distinguished themselves by mastering several disciplines, or areas of knowledge and expertise. Over time this led to the use of the words *Renaissance man* or *Renaissance woman* to describe a multitalented person. This did not happen, however, until the nineteenth century. During the actual Renaissance, the term for a multitalented person was *universal man*. Leonardo himself acknowledged the importance of striving for universal knowledge, clearly implying that it was one of his own chief goals.

Having no formal education, but gifted with a formidable intelligence, Renaissance artist Leonardo da Vinci became one of history's most revered artists.

Moreover, Leonardo felt that aiming for that goal was especially important for painters. "A painter is not admirable unless he is universal," he declared. He went on to explain that painters seek to reproduce any and all the creatures and objects of the natural world on their canvases. So they should study and become expert on as many of those things as possible. He stated:

> Since we know that painting embraces and includes in itself every object produced by nature or resulting from the fortuitous actions of men, in short, all that the eye can see, he seems to me but a poor master who can only do a figure well. For do you not perceive how many and various actions are performed by men only; how many different animals there are, as well as trees, plants, flowers, with many mountainous regions and plains, springs and rivers, cities with public and private buildings, machines, too, fit for the purposes of men, diverse costumes, decorations and arts? And all these things ought to be regarded as of equal importance and value, by the man who can be termed a good painter.[2]

## "The Fruit of Happiness"

Leonardo was not the first European to stress the importance of universal knowledge and strive for it. In fact, he consciously admired and modeled himself on the great Italian architect Leon Battista Alberti (born 1404), who died in 1472 when Leonardo was twenty. In addition to designing buildings, Alberti painted, sculpted, composed music, designed machines to raise sunken ships, and wrote both a play in Latin and the leading Renaissance book on architecture. In addition, he was a gifted athlete who some claimed could leap over a standing adult in a single bound. Alberti wrote, "Man is born . . . to work at large and magnificent tasks, thereby pleasing and honoring God, and manifesting in himself perfect virtue, that is, the fruit of happiness."[3]

Leonardo endeavored to create his own "fruit of happiness" by investigating, studying, and in some cases mastering a wide variety of subjects. The list includes painting, sculpture, music, architecture, mathematics, engineering, human anatomy, cartography (mapmaking), and botany. People in his own day were amazed at his versatility. Indeed, he appeared to be the greatest among many polymaths (multitalented people) who flourished within the remarkable intellectual and artistic layer of Renaissance society. The Italian painter and historian Giorgio Vasari (born 1511) was only one of many noted observers of the age who commented on Leonardo's gifts. In his biography of Leonardo, which is one of the key sources of information about him, Vasari wrote, "Sometimes, in supernatural fashion, beauty, grace, and talent are united beyond measure in one single person, in a manner that to whatever such a one turns his attention, his every action is so divine, that, surpassing all other men, it makes itself clearly known as a thing bestowed by God. . . . This was seen by all mankind in Leonardo da Vinci."[4]

# A Rock Star of the Arts

Well after Vasari's lifetime, Leonardo's high stature in the public consciousness of Western civilization did not diminish. Leonardo's most famous work, the *Mona Lisa*, remained an object of fascination and wonder. "No other painting in the world has been reproduced as often," one of the artist's modern biographers says. "No other attracts as many visitors or has been 'borrowed' by so many other artists."[5] By the middle of the nineteenth century, art scholar Roy McMullen writes, the *Mona Lisa* had become "a goal for pilgrimages and the object of a cult [of rabid fans]. It is decidedly not just a painting like other paintings. It might be better described . . . as a cross between a universal fetish [craze] and a Hollywood era film star."[6]

If the *Mona Lisa* can be designated a movie star, its creator would best be described as one of the rock stars of the fine arts world (along with his fellow Italian Michelangelo and a handful of others). Leonardo is still as big an object of wonder as his renowned painting. He is also a source of mystery. Various writers and conspiracy theorists have claimed that he hid secret

Leonardo's *Mona Lisa* is his most famous work. No other painting in the world has been reproduced more often or has attracted more visitors.

codes in his paintings and notebooks. Such theories have spawned numerous books and movies, which have contributed to making the name *da Vinci* a household word around the globe and among people of all ages.

The primary public fascination with Leonardo, however, was and remains the fact of his genius and versatility as an artist, thinker, and inventor. In scholar Stefan Klein's words:

How could one individual fuse within himself what appeared to be the knowledge of the entire world? . . . How was he able to create epoch-making paintings—and at the same time immerse himself in designing flying machines, robots, and all kinds of other devices and in contemplating a broad range of scientific questions? It seems miraculous that any one person could make his mark in so many areas in the course of a lifetime.[7]

The reasons Leonardo managed to accomplish so much in one lifetime are a matter of speculation and will likely never be known for certain. However, occasional remarks in his surviving writings suggest that he abhorred the idea of wasting even the smallest amount of time. To not utilize one's personal talents and energies at all times, he felt, would ensure that one would fail to make his or her mark in the world and be forgotten after death. According to one of his apprentices, Leonardo said, "He who . . . burns his life to waste leaves no more vestige of himself on earth than wind-blown smoke, or the foam upon the sea."[8] Leonardo followed his own advice. As a person, and especially as an artist, he more than made his mark, and he will never be forgotten.

# A Fantastically Fruitful Life

Leonardo da Vinci, whom later ages would acknowledge as one of the greatest artists in history, was born on April 15, 1452. The place was the small hill town called Vinci, then part of the territory of the northern Italian city-state of Florence. The baby's father was a young Florentine lawyer, Piero Fruosino di Antonio da Vinci, and his mother a peasant girl named Caterina. The unmarried parents did not stay together, as both married other people before the child's first birthday.

That birthday was recorded by Leonardo's grandfather, Antonio, in a note that a researcher discovered in Florence's official archives in 1939. It reads in part: "1452: There was born to me a grandson, the child of . . . Piero, my son, on April 15, a Saturday, at the third hour of the night. He bears the name Leonardo."[9] Like his father and grandfather, the baby received no surname (last, or family, name). The words *da Vinci* mean simply "from Vinci."

## The Star Apprentice

Almost nothing is known about Leonardo's childhood. He never mentioned his early years in his writings, perhaps because he had been an illegitimate child and did not want his adult acquaintances to know. For the first four or five years of his life, the boy stayed with his mother and stepfather, who had moved to Campo Zeppi, a hamlet within walking distance of Vinci.

At the end of that brief period, for reasons that remain obscure, Leonardo was living with his father and stepmother in the grandfather's house in Vinci. It is unknown whether the boy continued to see his mother from time to time after that. But most modern historians think he likely did. In the meantime Leonardo acquired an education, although it was informal and basic, probably administered by female relatives and maybe an occasional tutor. That it was somewhat inadequate is shown by the fact that he never mastered Latin. In those days instructors in formal schools tirelessly drilled Latin into their

Leonardo was born in Florence, Italy, on April 15, 1452. At the time, Florence (depicted in a fifteenth-century painting) was one of the most prosperous cities in Europe.

# A WORLD IN FLUX

*As former University of California scholar Ladislao Reti explains here, the traditional world of medieval Italy and Europe into which Leonardo was born was in the midst of flux, or change, a factor that colored his thinking and his art.*

Florence, scarcely 20 miles [32.18km] away from Vinci, Leonardo's birthplace, was at this time the richest city in Europe. Bankers and wool merchants had produced a stable economic basis upon which healthy merchant and craftsmen classes could be built. In addition, Florence, a republic for thirty years when Leonardo was born, had been governed by humanist leaders who believed in the dignity of [humanity] and the possibility of achieving happiness through the application of intelligence. . . . Scientific developments were also connected with the changes in Leonardo's world. For example, the improvement and increased use of cannon and gunpowder drastically altered the concepts of . . . armored battle. [Similarly] Copernican astronomy [showing that Earth revolves around the sun] changed [humanity's] perspective of [itself] and [its] world in relation to the universe. [Johannes] Gutenberg's invention of the printing press [was] perhaps the most devastating blow to [medieval traditions], opening up literature, science, art, philosophy—anything that could be written—to the common [person].

Ladislao Reti, ed. *The Unknown Leonardo.* New York: Abradale, 1990, p. 11.

students. The young man did learn some mathematics, which later proved useful to him.

At some point in his youth, Leonardo demonstrated his artistic talent to his father. According to Giorgio Vasari, a biographer of the late Renaissance, the boy "never ceased drawing" the things around him, and his duly impressed father "one day took some of his drawings and carried them to Andrea del Verrocchio." Verrocchio was a Florentine sculptor and painter who ran a successful studio and regularly took in and trained apprentices. Piero asked Verrocchio "whether Leonardo, by devoting himself to drawing," might one day make a living at it. In Vasari's words, the sculptor "was astonished" at the boy's talent and "urged Piero that he should make him study it."[10]

This was how, in 1466 at age fourteen, Leonardo became Verrocchio's apprentice. For a young man used to life in villages and small towns, the move to Florence, one of Italy's busiest and most attractive cities, must have been exciting. Adding to the thrill, no doubt, was the fact that he would now receive formal training in a number of trades and disciplines, including plaster casting, metalworking, carpentry, drawing, painting, and sculpture. "As an apprentice," researcher Robert Wallace explains,

> Leonardo doubtless followed the standard routine, commencing with the grinding of colors [paint pigments] and other drudgery and then, as his skills increased, gradually being allowed to execute the simpler parts of whatever work Verrocchio happened to have in hand. Much of what he learned must have come from the master himself, but there were more advanced pupils or assistants in the shop, notably Pietro Perugino, six years older than Leonardo, from whom he may have learned basic techniques. In his turn, Leonardo obviously helped and influenced younger apprentices, such as Lorenzo di Credi, whose style eventually became so slavishly "Leonardoesque" that it sometimes requires an expert eye to tell their works apart.[11]

The nature of most of the projects Leonardo worked on during his years with Verrocchio is uncertain. However, a few have been identified by modern experts, including some work on Verrocchio's painting *Tobias and the Angel*. In those days, as Wallace says, major artists allowed their leading apprentices to execute small sections of the works their studios turned out. It is now generally accepted that Leonardo painted the fish held by Tobias in the picture and maybe the dog running behind the angel.

It appears that Verrocchio, recognizing the young man's extraordinary talent, eventually allowed him to tackle more formidable projects. Sometime in his late teens, according to Vasari, Leonardo painted substantial parts of his master's *Baptism of Christ*. The younger man's brushstrokes are indeed recognizable in the figure of the young angel holding Jesus's garment and in much of the figure of Jesus as well. In addition, some evidence suggests that Verrocchio at times used Leonardo, said to be an unusually handsome youth, as a model. A number of art historians think that the face of Verrocchio's statue of the biblical character David was fashioned after that of his star apprentice.

## Striking Out on His Own

Leonardo showed so much promise, in fact, that when he was only twenty (in 1472), both his father and painting master felt he was ready to strike out on his own. In that year the young man was granted the status of master, or skilled professional, by Florence's prestigious Guild of St. Luke, an organization of independent artists and doctors. Also, Piero da Vinci arranged for his talented son to have his own workshop. At first, however, Leonardo felt more comfortable continuing to work on projects with Verrocchio, with whom he had developed a strong friendship. It was not until 1478 that the younger artist began accepting major commissions for artworks on his own.

The first of these independent projects that Leonardo accepted was the creation of an altarpiece, or decoration for a church altar, for Florence's Chapel of St. Bernard (which he never fully conceptualized or finished). He also began work on a large panel painting (a painting on a wooden panel) for the monastery of San Donato a Scopeto in 1481. Titled *Adoration of the Magi*, its subject was the infant Jesus in his manger, accompanied by his mother, Mary. Unlike most painted manger scenes, which are small-scale and intimate, Leonardo's was large-scale and busy, with dozens of shepherds, visitors, angels, and other figures milling about behind the central mother and child. These figures, including a shepherd whose face is likely a self-portrait of the artist, are plainly visible in the initial drawing he did on the panel.

The work never progressed any further, however, because in 1482 Leonardo abruptly left Florence and journeyed to Milan, lying 156 miles (251km) to the northwest. Another bustling Italian center of trade and the arts, Milan was then ruled by Duke Lodovico Sforza (also known as Lodovico il Moro), an autocratic leader but dedicated patron of the arts. It is not completely clear why the young man made the move. But the post he accepted was that of official artist for the

Leonardo's *Adoration of the Magi* was started in 1481 for the monastery of San Donato a Scopeto in Florence. He left it unfinished when he moved to Milan in 1482.

While in the employ of Duke Lodovico Sforza, Leonardo painted *Lady with an Ermine*; the subject is believed to be the duke's mistress, Cecilia Gallerani.

duke's court. It may be that Leonardo hoped the huge financial backing and prestige of the Sforza family would provide him with opportunities he could not find elsewhere. He also may have been attracted by rumors that Milan's ruler was looking for someone to create an enormous sculpture of a horse. Landing such an assignment was guaranteed to make any artist famous and in demand throughout Europe.

To get the coveted post in Lodovico's court, Leonardo composed a letter containing what is today often termed a *résumé*. Clearly intended to impress the duke, it claimed that the applicant for the position was capable of much more than just painting pretty pictures. It was well known that the duke was not only an arts supporter, but also a military man interested in expanding Milan's influence, if necessary by force. So in the résumé, Leonardo stressed that he was capable of fashioning all manner of effective defensive and offensive weapons. He said in part:

> I have [invented] many machines most efficient for [military] offense and defense, and vessels which will resist the attack of the largest guns and powder and fumes. . . . In case of [your] need, I will make big guns, mortars, [but] where the operation of bombardment might fail, I would contrive catapults. . . . In time of peace I [can design] buildings, public and private. [In addition] I can carry out sculpture in marble, bronze, and clay, and I also can do in painting whatever may [need to] be done. . . . If any of the above-mentioned things seem to anyone to be impossible . . . I am most ready to [demonstrate them] in whatever place may please your Excellency.[12]

# A Capable Writer and Musician

Painting, sculpture, architecture, and military engineering were not the only talents and services that Leonardo could offer Lodovico or any other potential boss. The gifted young man was also a capable writer and musician. By this time Leonardo had already begun to compile the huge mass of detailed notes that centuries later would be collected and published as his so-called notebooks. It appears that he expected to publish them himself, and it remains unclear why he never did so. He set down most of these writings using his now famous "mirror writing," in which he wrote backward, requiring one to look at an image in a mirror to read it. The reason for this approach was different than many people today assume. According to one modern expert on Leonardo, the artist was

> left-handed, and throughout his life he habitually wrote [his notes] in mirror-image, from right to left. This was not an attempt to keep his researches secret, as has been claimed, for Leonardo's mirror-writing is relatively easy to read with a little patience. Mirror-writing is a common developmental quirk in child-hood, and what may have begun as an entertaining trick became a habit that Leonardo never had cause to discard.[13]

Leonardo also learned to use mirrors to help him become a better judge or critic of his own paintings while he was work-ing on them. He explained in his notes:

> We know very well that errors are better recognized in the works of others than in our own, and that often, while [finding] little faults in others, you may ignore great ones in yourself. To avoid such ignorance . . . I say that when you paint you should have a flat mirror and often look at your work as reflected in it, when you will see it reversed, and it will appear to you like some other painter's work, so you will be better able to judge of its faults than in any other way.[14]

In addition, Leonardo somehow found the time to learn to play several musical instruments, including the lyre, a small harp popular in ancient and medieval times. He also designed a number of new instruments. (The violin was not, as claimed by some early modern biographers, one of them.) These included some flute-like devices and a complex keyboard instrument with strings, which was never actually built and used by anyone. As researcher Maxine Annabell points out, Leonardo also found clever ways to improve existing instruments. He "created a mechanism which would allow drummers to tighten or slacken skins with one hand and move the drumsticks using a system of cogs . . . and designed improved mechanisms for keyboards so they would be easier to play."[15]

# Travels Through Italy

Having landed the position with Duke Lodovico, Leonardo ended up living and working in Milan from 1482 to 1499, a period of seventeen years in which he was almost constantly busy. Although his official role was that of court painter, Lodovico employed him on many other kinds of projects. Among them were designing elaborate decorations for feasts and weddings held by the duke and his leading nobles and helping to plan new additions to the Milan Cathedral (the Duomo di Milano). Lodovico also assigned Leonardo the creation of a giant equestrian (horse-shaped) statue, proving that the earlier rumors about such a project had been true.

While drawing sketches for the great statue's design and working on a clay model of it, Leonardo spent much of his time engaging in his chief profession—painting. The first major painting he did under Duke Lodovico's sponsorship was his initial version of the *Virgin of the Rocks*. Completed in 1486, it is nearly identical to a second version the artist began in Milan in 1495. (The reason he did two separate versions remains unclear.) Leonardo also painted a large mural for Lodovico—*The Last Supper*, finished in 1498, which became one of the artist's two most famous works.

Not long after completing *The Last Supper*, Leonardo was forced to leave Milan. In 1499 Duke Lodovico was defeated by an invading French army, which seized control of the city. Leonardo fled to Venice, in northeastern Italy, and in the following year

*One of Leonardo's modern biographers, Robert Payne, here comments on the great artist's humanity, pointing out how thoughtful and courteous he was to people, even the dead and those he did not know well or at all.*

An old man, a centenarian [someone 100 years old or older], died in the hospital where [Leonardo] was working. Leonardo talked to him during his last hours and discovered that he had never had a day's illness. Immediately after the man died, Leonardo [who had obtained the man's permission to dissect him after his death] began to cut him up in the hope of learning what changes in the physical body bring about death. At the top of the first page of his anatomical study of the old man, he drew, with grave courtesy, a portrait of the man as he was when alive. It was Leonardo's salute to the memory of the living man, while he was engaged in dismembering the corpse. His life was made up of such acts of courtesy.

Robert Payne. *Leonardo.* Garden City, NY: Doubleday, 1978, p. xvi.

returned to his native Florence. There he was greeted as a celebrity and provided with a spacious workshop by the monks of a local monastery. According to Vasari, that workshop was where Leonardo did the cartoon, or preliminary full-sized drawing, for an ultimately unfinished painting titled *The Virgin and Child with St. Anne*. (Some modern experts think Vasari was wrong and that the cartoon was done shortly before the artist left Milan.)

In 1502 the restless Leonardo headed to Cesena, about halfway between Florence and Venice. There he entered the

During the time he worked for Duke Lodovico, Leonardo created his first major painting, *Virgin of the Rocks*, in 1486.

service of Cesare (CHES-a-ray) Borgia, son of Pope Alexander VI and a member of a notorious family of political schemers. As a military engineer for his new boss, Leonardo traveled widely through the Italian peninsula. Borgia was extremely impressed with him and trusted him with important assignments, including inspecting and maintaining the several Borgia-controlled forts. A surviving document signed by Borgia himself gave Leonardo safe passage to carry out his inspections. It reads in part:

> Our most excellent and well-beloved friend, the architect and engineer . . . Leonardo Vinci . . . shall be given free passage and be relieved of all public tax, both for himself and his party, and shall be welcomed amicably, and may make measurements and examine whatever he pleases. . . . It is our will that every engineer in our dominions shall be bound to confer with him and follow his advice. And let no man dare to do the contrary, if he does not wish to incur our extreme displeasure.[16]

## Scientific Studies

For reasons unknown, in 1503 Leonardo left Borgia's employ and went back to Florence. There the artist worked on a huge mural—*The Battle of Anghiari*, still another project he left unfinished. It appears that he also began working on the *Mona Lisa*, by far his most renowned artwork.

By 1508 Leonardo had moved back to Milan, where at age fifty-six he found himself devoting more and more time to his scientific studies, which he had carried out off and on during most of his adult life. Among others, these included studies of botany, mechanics, the nature of flight, and human anatomy. In all of these studies he backed up his conclusions and theories with numerous drawings, many of them elaborate and detailed. Some show primitive helicopters and glider planes, parachutes, battleships, submarines, steam-powered weapons, and what appear to be robots, all devices that were centuries ahead of their time. Perhaps the most impressive of Leonardo's

Upon returning to Florence as a celebrated artist in 1500, Leonardo painted his work *Virgin and Child with Saint Anne.*

sketches were his anatomical renderings. In the words of a leading modern medical historian:

> No one before him . . . made so many dissections on human bodies, nor did any understand so well how to interpret the findings. His account of the uterus was far more accurate . . . than any that preceded him. He was the first to give a correct description of the human skeleton . . . of the vertebral column, [and] practically all the muscles of the human body. No one before him had drawn the nerves and the blood vessels even approximately as correctly as he . . . nor had anyone before him [drawn] that wealth of anatomical details which he observed.[17]

In 1513 Giuliano de' Medici, brother of Pope Leo X, invited Leonardo to live and work in the Vatican, the pope's residence in Rome. Not much is known about what the aging artist-scientist did there, but most historians agree that he was not very happy with his situation. So when his newest mentor, Giuliano, died in 1516, Leonardo accepted another invitation to move, this one from France's King Francis I. The king set Leonardo up in an elegant manor house, Clos Lucé, close by the monarch's own residence in Amboise, in west-central France. The artist also received a substantial pension to pay for his expenses and enjoyed the companionship of Francesco Melzi, an apprentice and close friend since 1506. Having never married or had any children, Leonardo seems to have viewed Melzi, another longtime assistant named Salai, and a few other former apprentices as his immediate family.

Leonardo was by now in his mid-sixties and suffering from some physical problems. The proof for this comes from a surviving document written by Antonio de Beatis, the secretary of a Catholic cardinal who visited the aging artist-scholar at Clos Lucé in October 1517. Beatis wrote, "One cannot expect any more good [painting] work from him, as a certain paralysis has crippled his right hand. [But] although Mr. Leonardo can no longer paint with the sweetness which was peculiar to him, he can still design [artworks] and instruct others."[18]

*Leonardo's longtime pupil and friend, Francesco Melzi wrote the following passage shortly after his master's passing in 1519.*

He was to me the best of fathers, and it is impossible for me to express the grief that his death has caused me. Until the day when my body is laid under the ground, I shall experience perpetual sorrow, and not without reason, for he daily showed me the most devoted and warmest affection. His loss is a grief to everyone, for it is not in the power of nature to reproduce another such man. May the Almighty accord him everlasting rest. He passed from the present life on the 2nd of May with all the sacraments of holy Mother Church and will be disposed to receive them.

Quoted in Ludwig Goldsheider. *Leonardo da Vinci*. New York: Phaidon, 1959, p. 39.

*Upon Leonardo's death, his longtime assistant and pupil Francesco Melzi (pictured) wrote eloquently of his master's passing.*

The end of Leonardo's fantastically fruitful life came on May 2, 1519. According to Vasari, King Francis, who had recently become close to the artist, gently held his head in his arms as he died. (Some historians argue that Francis was far away when Leonardo passed on and therefore did not witness the event. But others accept Vasari's version, so the king's presence at the deathbed remains a matter of debate.)

Crushed by the loss of his longtime friend and mentor, Melzi inherited most of Leonardo's paintings, art materials, books, and other personal belongings. In a letter to the dead man's surviving blood relatives (some half-brothers born to Piero da Vinci and his several wives), Melzi delivered what most experts today view as a fitting epitaph for an individual whose talents exceeded those of nearly all other people in history. "It is not in the power of nature to reproduce another such man," Melzi wrote. "May the Almighty accord him everlasting rest."[19]

# The Paintings Executed Before 1490

I n spite of his brilliance and accomplishments in a wide range of arts and intellectual disciplines, including several sciences, Leonardo was first and foremost a painter. In addition to creating some of history's most famous paintings, he influenced numerous artists, both in his own generation and in later ones. This tremendous historical influence was based on a surprisingly small number of works. Art experts have identified fewer than twenty paintings that can definitely be attributed to his hand, several of them unfinished. Moreover, some of these paintings were produced when he was still a young man assisting his master, Verrocchio. The fact that Leonardo's huge reputation as a painter rests mainly on only a handful of his more mature works speaks volumes about his nearly unmatched artistic inventiveness and skill.

There were several reasons that Leonardo turned out so few finished paintings. The principal one was the large amount of time he invested in planning and preparation for each project, including research and reams of preliminary sketches and notes. According to one of his leading modern biographers, Serge Bramly:

Leonardo's well-known slowness and the small number of his works were the result . . . of the trouble he took over the conception of each work. He never began a painting until he had thoroughly mastered his subject. He was incapable of repeating what had already been done by someone else, and only took up his brushes once a revolution in the mind had been accomplished. A radical innovator, a thinker, and a perfectionist, he left infinitely more studies and notes than any other Renaissance artist.[20]

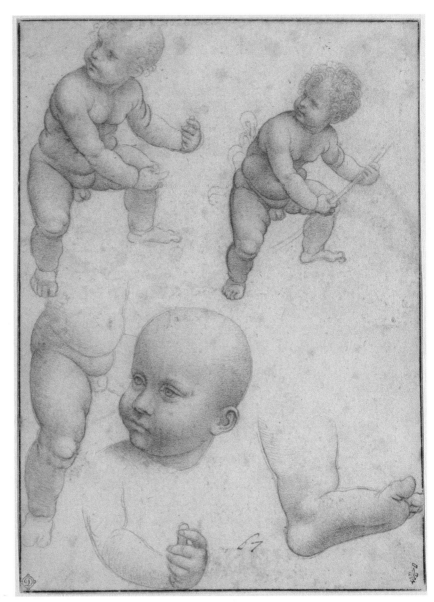

Leonardo spent long hours doing research and making preliminary sketches in preparation for each of his works. Shown here are six studies of an infant in three-quarter view.

In addition to their originality and perfection of execution, Leonardo's paintings were and remain remarkable for their striking portrayal of the human form. This can be discerned in the works he did in his first broad painting period, before 1490, and his later one, encompassing the years after that date. His characters almost always seem to be filled with an inner energy and display distinct emotional expressions. These attributes are most famously associated with his *Mona Lisa* but can be seen in his other paintings, too. As noted art historian Elke Linda Buchholz puts it, "His compositions produce an extraordinarily lively effect and appear harmonic and flowing. Typically, Leonardo created very fine modulations [variations] of light and shadow, especially with faces and background landscapes. His human beings express finely differentiated feelings. In creating these figures, he always strove for ideal beauty."[21]

# The *Baptism of Christ*

Those qualities—expert use of light and shadow and lucid depiction of the inner feelings of human subjects—are clearly visible even in Leonardo's earliest paintings. Earliest of all, at least among those in which he did a substantial portion of the work, was the *Baptism of Christ*. Produced by Verrocchio's studio, it was commissioned in about 1470 by the monks of the San Salvi monastery, lying just outside of Florence. It shows Jesus, wearing a loincloth, standing in the center of the picture, with two angels kneeling to the viewer's left. Jesus's cousin, John the Baptist, looms to the right, in the midst of anointing Jesus's head with water from the Jordan River.

Modern experts have closely studied the work, analyzing its brushstrokes, which are unique to each artist, and subtle uses of color and light. Their general consensus is that Verrocchio painted an initial version of the work in 1490 using tempera. Before the mid-Renaissance (circa 1450–1500), nearly all European painters used this type of paint, made by mixing powdered pigments with egg yoke, water, or some other liquid, and a small amount of glue to make sure the paint would stick to the painting surface.

In Andrea del Verrocchio's 1472 painting *Baptism of Christ,* his young assistant Leonardo is generally thought to have painted the angel on the left.

Thanks to extensive experiments by a few inventive Dutch artists, however, oil-based paints rapidly supplanted tempera in the late 1400s and early 1500s. Dutchman Jan van Eyck (born circa 1395), who perfected the oil-painting medium, demonstrated that using oil allowed an artist to produce more intricate detail than was possible with tempera. This was because oil paint takes longer to dry, so a painter has considerably more time to add detail or make changes.

Although it is difficult to tell for sure, the transition from tempera to oil seems to have occurred in Verrocchio's workshop in the early 1470s. More certain is that in about 1472 the *Baptism of Christ* painting underwent a facelift. Most of the work, which had been painted in tempera on a wooden panel, was over-painted with oils. Moreover, it appears certain that Leonardo, then about twenty, was responsible for many of the additions. Experts can recognize his unique hand in several sections of the picture. In particular, the angel at the far left in the revised version is completely Leonardo's and in fact quite different in appearance from Verrocchio's version. "An x-ray of this painting showed that the original sketching Verrocchio did for Leonardo's angel was entirely different from the final result," Maxine Annabell points out. "This shows that even at this early stage he was freeing himself of his master's coaching to follow his own path. It's interesting to compare the two angels, Leonardo's paying close attention to the action, the figure looking quite natural and part of the activities. In contrast, Verrocchio's angel stares off into space with no interest in what is going on, he looks entirely bored."[22]

The other sections of the painting that Leonardo redid in oils included parts of Jesus's body, including his torso and the heavy eyelids that give his face such a poignant, or emotionally touching, expression. Leonardo also "radically altered the landscape in the distance," art historian Jack Wasserman comments. He "brought the water forward from the middle ground so that it eddies around Christ's feet. In so doing, he had perhaps hoped to disguise the [disjointed break] between the middle distance and the foreground of the [original] painting, thereby unifying them."[23]

# From *Annunciation* to *Adoration*

Leonardo contributed to other painting projects while working in Verrocchio's studio in the 1470s. One that has been verified as partially his is among two pictures titled *The Annunciation* produced by the studio in that decade. In Western religious literature and art, the Annunciation is the moment when an angel tells the biblical Mary that she will soon conceive a divine child. Both versions created by Verrocchio's assistants show the angel kneeling at the left and reaching out with its right hand toward Mary, who sits at the right. They are on a stone terrace overlooking a distant landscape of small seaports and ships floating near them.

One of the two paintings, now in the Louvre Museum in Paris, is clearly not Leonardo's, and experts still debate which of Verrocchio's helpers executed it. The other work, which hangs in Florence's Uffizi Gallery, was for a long time attributed to another painter but has since been shown to be partly done by Leonardo. The consensus of experts is that he contributed the overall design and painted parts of the angel and all of the background landscape. The rest of the picture seems to have been done by other members of Verrocchio's in-house staff.

The first major painting that Leonardo attempted on his own was the *Adoration of the Magi*, commissioned in 1481 by the monastery of San Donato a Scopeto. *Attempted* is the operative word here, because he never finished the work. All that has survived on the original wooden panel is a monochromatic (colorless or single-colored) initial drawing, to which the artist intended to add paint. Still, it is more than a mere cartoon. Leonardo took the next step beyond mere line drawing and blocked in most of the light and shadowed areas, giving much of the panel a three-dimensional look.

The most striking aspect of the work is the controlled chaos, so to speak, of the masses of human figures surrounding Jesus and Mary, who dominate the center foreground. In addition to the Magi (the famous three foreign kings bearing gifts for Jesus), there are shepherds, soldiers, angels, and others. They display a wide range and depth of emotions, including wonder, curiosity, devotion, joy, and contemplation. No painter before Leonardo had tried to portray so many and varied emotions in a single painting. "Only Leonardo," one scholar writes, recognized the potential of showing numerous "powerful and identifiable emotions and raised them to such a level of universality that they inspire in the beholder comparable feelings of awe and devotion."[24]

Another important aspect of the *Adoration of the Magi* is Leonardo's depiction of horses. They can be seen running and rearing up in the background as their riders engage in jousting matches. For years before beginning this work, Leonardo had been fascinated by horses and had studied and sketched them standing, walking, trotting, and rearing up on their hind legs. In this and later paintings, he demonstrated that these studies had paid off. No other Renaissance artist surpassed him in representing horses; moreover, no other artist of the period could match him in capturing the look, dynamics, and tensions of combat, both with and without horses.

While working at Verrocchio's studio Leonardo participated in painting *The Annunciation*. Modern scholars think he did most of the painting.

## St. Jerome and the Lion

Evidence suggests that Leonardo began work on the *Adoration of the Magi* sometime between 1481 and 1482, shortly before he left Florence to work for Duke Lodovico in Milan. It was not the only painting that he left unfinished from that short but fruitful period. He also began and never completed another panel painting, this one portraying the well-known biblical character St. Jerome. Like *Magi*, *St. Jerome in the Desert* has survived in a brownish monochromatic drawing in which most of the shading has been added in preparation for adding the colored pigments.

Leonardo's painting of St. Jerome, one of his most dramatic and popular works, underwent a torturous existence in the centuries following its creator's death. For a while the Vatican, home and office of the Catholic pope, kept it safe. But later the artwork passed into the possession of a woman named Angelica Kaufmann. Somehow during her period of ownership it got lost, and an unknown individual, not realizing its worth, cut it into two pieces. One section became a tabletop, and a shoemaker used the other section as part of a stool. A Catholic cardinal named Joseph Fesch recognized the painting on the tabletop in 1820. Over time he managed to find the other piece, and the painting was restored. Today it rests in the Vatican in Rome.

*Leonardo's* Saint Jerome in the Wilderness *was cut into two pieces and separated, but in 1820 Cardinal Joseph Fesch, an art collector, found both pieces and had the painting reassembled.*

Despite its lack of full color, the composition and figures in *St. Jerome* are clear enough to show that it is one of Leonardo's most dramatic scenes. As Robert Payne describes it:

> We see St. Jerome kneeling beside a lion, one arm out-flung, gazing penitently and adoringly at a crucifix. He is naked except for a cloak falling loosely over his left shoulder. He is very old and the deeply lined face and emaciated [very thin] body have the dignity of age. Behind him lies the desert with the strange bulbous rocks that [also] appear in the *Adoration of the Magi* in the distance, while closer at hand . . . is a heap of rocks and what appears to be the entrance of a grotto [cave] where the saint spent the better part of his life. One imagines that a cry has just escaped from the saint's lips. The lion's mouth is open, and he is roaring.[25]

The gaunt figure of St. Jerome in this highly theatrical picture reflects Leonardo's studies in human anatomy, which he had recently begun. Among other things, his studies involved creating detailed drawings of body parts he observed during the dissection of corpses. In this manner, the young man had become quite familiar with the bones and muscles of the body, and some of what he had learned can be seen in Jerome's almost skeletal appearance.

The saint's figure is reminiscent not only of Leonardo's anatomical drawings, but also of other sketches he had been doing of disfigured and/or odd-looking people he sometimes encountered on street corners and elsewhere. Vasari referred to Leonardo's interest in the bizarre, saying that he was

> so delighted when he saw curious[-looking human] heads . . . that he would follow about anyone who had thus attracted his attention for a whole day, acquiring such a clear idea of him that when he went home he would draw the head as well as if the man had been present. In this way, many heads of men and women came to be drawn, and I have several such pen-and-ink drawings in my [possession].[26]

Another important aspect of *St. Jerome* is the lion in the foreground. A number of art historians and critics have remarked over the years that in spite of its lack of detail in the preliminary drawing, the image is sleek, well-proportioned, and very believable. There was a good reason for this expertise in depicting lions. Although the horse may well have been Leonardo's favorite beast, he also had a deep-seated interest in many other animals, especially the lion. His admiration for lions and what he perceived as their courage can be seen in a remark from his notebooks: "The lion is never afraid, but rather fights with a bold spirit and savage onslaught against a multitude of hunters, always seeking to injure the first that injures him."[27]

Leonardo visited and studied several lions that were kept in a so-called lion house in Florence during his childhood and early adulthood. During a nostalgic moment much later in life, when he was in his sixties, he drew the lion house from memory. His notebooks also contain a reference to lions in captivity that he may have learned about firsthand: "We see the most striking example of humility in the lamb which will submit to any animal; and when they are given for food to imprisoned lions they are as gentle to them as to their own mother, so that very often it has been seen that the lions forbear to kill them."[28]

## The Mystery of the Cave

*St. Jerome* also contains an interesting visual metaphor involving lions. In the wild the now extinct European species of these creatures were known to dwell in caves sometimes. The fact that Jerome also lived in a cave, which the artist included in the picture, gives the saint a sort of shared brotherhood with the beast.

Another major painting from the first two decades of Leonardo's artistic career depicts a cave. Frequently called his most original painting, as well as his strangest and most puzzling work, it is titled *The Madonna of the Rocks* (sometimes translated into English as *The Virgin of the Rocks*). It dates to around 1483 to 1485, which means it was created during Leonardo's early years in Milan. "The painting is a mysterious

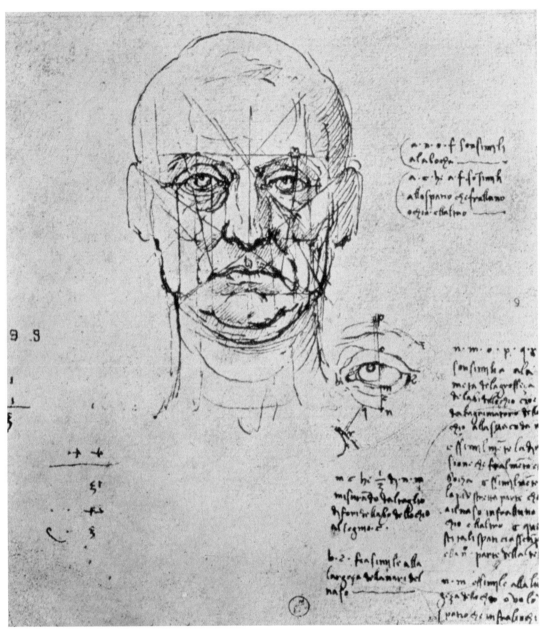

revelation," one modern expert writes, "with a setting that is not of this earth, a watery cave, open to the sky, sheltering the Virgin [Mary], the infants [Jesus] and John [the Baptist], and an angel. . . . The figures are supremely graceful and at ease, and the details of plant life are as true to nature as the most skilled botanical artist could draw them."[29]

Leonardo's sketches of a human face and eye reveal his astute observations of human physical characteristics.

The painting is indeed baffling in its unusual imagery, most of it apparently symbolic, or standing for other things. The question that generations of observers have often asked is: What are those other things? Why, for instance, does the angel point emphatically at baby John rather than at Jesus? Or is the child whom Mary touches with her right hand really John after all? Might he instead be a representation of humanity in general, which the New Testament of the Bible says Jesus saved by dying on the cross? People have also conjectured that the cave might be symbolic of a mystical womb, since Jesus had recently come from Mary's womb through divine intervention.

No one has ever been able to answer these and other such questions about *The Madonna of the Rocks*. After all, Robert Wallace points out, Leonardo, "like most great painters, never made the slightest effort to explain this or any other of his works."[30] One possible explanation of Leonardo's use of the cave that scholars have offered over the years is that he was long haunted by an experience he had had in a real cave when he was a young man. He described part of it in a passage from his notebooks, saying:

> Having wandered some distance among gloomy rocks, I came to the entrance of a great cavern, in front of which I stood some time, astonished and unaware of such a thing. Bending my back into an arch I rested my left hand on my knee and held my right hand over my down-cast and contracted eye brows. Often [I bent] first one way and then the other, to see whether I could discover anything inside, [but] this [was] forbidden by the deep darkness within. . . . After having remained there some time, two contrary emotions arose in me, fear and desire—fear of the threatening dark cavern, [and] desire to see whether there were any marvelous things within it.[31]

What Leonardo intended the cave, the pointing finger, and other visual images to mean will likely never be known. What is more certain is that *The Madonna of the Rocks* was the

*A great many art critics and historians have described Leonardo's* Madonna of the Rocks *over the centuries. One of the more atmospheric and effective portrayals of the painting was by Leonardo's biographer Antonina Vallentin.*

*A* strange darkness fills the grotto in which the Virgin is kneeling. Shadows play amid the dank and trickling cliffs, and the plants and stones glisten mysteriously in the velvety hollow, which suddenly opens out to admit the entrance of light in the far distance. These rocky ledges that overhang the darkness of the hollow, this medley of flowers springing from the rich moss, might equally well be the resting-place of heathen gods. Light-footed nymphs might emerge in alarm from the golden twilight, fleeing from the god Pan in this enchanted wilderness. There is more, too, of a heathen god than a heavenly messenger in the angel who has come down by the side of the Christ Child, the flaming red stain of

his garment spreading out as he suddenly kneels. An ecstatic [thrilled] glance comes from his almond-shaped eyes between their fleshy and sensual lids, a glance laden with mystery.

Antonina Vallentin. *Leonardo da Vinci: The Tragic Pursuit of Perfection.* Translated by E.W. Dicks. New York: Viking, 1938, pp. 97–98.

*Leonardo's* Madonna of the Rocks.

last major painting he did before 1490. For most artists, past and present, turning out a painting as finely wrought as *The Madonna of the Rocks*, or even the unfinished *Adoration of the Magi*, would be enough to create a major reputation. But Leonardo was destined for greater things. Beginning in the 1490s, he managed to outdo his younger self by producing some of the most sublime and famous artworks of all time.

# The Paintings Produced After 1490

A rt critics both in Leonardo's own day and in later ages have agreed that he produced his greatest paintings between about 1490 and 1513. This period encompassed about half of his initial stay in Milan, in the employ of Duke Lodovico; his residence in his home city of Florence from 1503 to 1508; and his second stay in Milan, from 1508 to 1513. As had been the case in the past, for one reason or another Leonardo left some of his post-1490 paintings unfinished. Yet even those that have survived only as preliminary drawings or cartoons are widely viewed as superb artworks. Moreover, those pictures he did finish, including *The Last Supper*, *Mona Lisa*, and *Salvator Mundi*, are universally acclaimed as among the greatest paintings in history.

One reason for the high quality of Leonardo's later paintings is that he was constantly experimenting with new ideas and approaches intended to make his works look more realistic and effective. This research resulted in the development of two techniques that revolutionized the art of painting. The first was aerial perspective. When still a young man, Leonardo noticed that the farther away an object is from a viewer, the more its hue shifts toward the blue end of the spectrum. (This is because over a distance Earth's atmosphere variously absorbs and scatters the colors making up white light.) Leonardo also noticed that over a distance the atmosphere appears increasingly hazy-looking. His depiction of these atmospheric effects in his background landscapes became known as aerial perspective.

The second important technique he developed is called sfumato (from the Italian word *sfumare*, meaning "to shade"). It is, as one expert says, "a fine, almost unnoticeable blur found especially over facial features, but also over landscapes. In this way, Leonardo avoided the over-sharp precision and stiffness of earlier portraiture. Tones blend into one another, and the

landscape melds with the human figure, the cosmos with humanity."[32] Leonardo used these and other techniques to great effect in a number of his later works, with particularly stunning results in his masterpieces the *Mona Lisa* and *The Last Supper*.

## "So Absorbed Was He in His Work"

The latter work, depicting the final meal shared by Jesus with his twelve disciples, was requested by Duke Lodovico. He wanted it to adorn the north wall of the dining hall of Milan's

In *The Last Supper*, Leonardo employed new techniques that involved the use of perspective and shading to add depth to his work. He worked on his seminal masterpiece for six years.

Church of Santa Maria delle Grazie, which was to be his burial place. The plan was for an unusually large mural, measuring 30 by 14 feet (9m by 4.3m), clearly a challenge for any painter. Rising to that challenge, Leonardo, per usual a perfectionist, spent nearly three years doing preliminary studies and drawings. He began applying the paint in 1495 and completed the mural in late 1497 or early 1498. An eyewitness account of the actual creation of this renowned picture has survived. Italian writer Matteo Bandello visited the dining hall on several occasions as the work progressed and later recalled:

> He [Leonardo] would often come to the [church] at early dawn. And this I have seen him do myself. Hastily mounting the scaffold, he worked diligently until the shades of evening compelled him to cease, never thinking to take food at all, so absorbed was he in his work. At other times he would remain there three or four days without touching his picture, only coming for a few hours to remain before it, with folded arms, gazing at his figures as if to criticize them himself. At midday, too, when the glare of the sun at its zenith had made barren all the streets of Milan, I have seen him hasten from the citadel, where he was [working on a sculpture for the duke], without seeking shade, by the shortest way to the [church], where he would add a touch or two [to the painting] and immediately return [to the citadel].[33]

The seemingly endless days of hard work that Bandello witnessed paid off. The monks were amazed by the degree of realism Leonardo had imparted to the figures in the picture, as were all others who saw it in its original state. Everyone agreed that the painting also beautifully captured the emotions of the men portrayed. Vasari, who viewed it only a few years after the artist's death, wrote:

> Leonardo imagined and succeeded in expressing that anxiety which had seized the disciples in wishing to

know who should betray their Master. For that reason, in all their faces are seen love, fear, and wrath, or rather, sorrow, at not being able to understand the meaning of Christ . . . not to mention that every least part of the work displays an incredible diligence, seeing that even in the tablecloth the texture of the stuff is [painted] in such a manner that [actual] linen itself could not seem more real.[34]

Regrettably, Vasari also noticed that the picture's paint was already beginning to fade and chip away. The chief culprit, it turned out, was moisture, as the combination of tempera and oil that Leonardo had employed proved unable to withstand the room's high humidity. To make matters worse, as the colors continued to fade, the painting suffered one added humiliation after another. In the words of one expert observer:

*Leonardo made many preliminary drawings for The Last Supper.*

In 1652, after serious deterioration had set in, a door was cut through the center of the wall. The effects of this are still clearly visible across the bottom of the painted tablecloth and at Christ's place. His feet were cut off in the process. In 1796, the refectory was used as a stable by French troops. [Their commander], Napoleon, gave strict orders that no damage was to be done but the disciples [in the painting] were pelted with clay. Later still, the room was used for storing hay and, as if the fates had decided to finish the work off, in 1800 a flood covered the entire painting with green mold.[35]

A number of attempts were made over the centuries to repair and/or refurbish *The Last Supper*. Most of these were inadequate or even made matters worse. A final, valiant effort was completed in 1954 by master art restorer Mauro Pellicioli. Thanks to him, though most of Leonardo's original paint, along with the expressions on the disciples' faces, are gone forever, visitors can get at least a rough idea of what the work originally looked like.

# From St. Anne to the Dust of Battle

Not long after finishing *The Last Supper* and shortly before or after he left Milan in 1499, Leonardo began work on *The Virgin and Child with St. Anne*. Commissioned by the monks of Florence's Santissima Annunziata Church for their high altar, *The Virgin and Child* was to show a grouping of the Virgin Mary; her mother, St. Anne; and the infants Jesus and St. John. Leonardo did a number of sketches for the work, as well as a cartoon ready for painting. But no paint ever touched this initial conception of the work. For reasons that are unclear, the artist abandoned it. The cartoon, today usually called the Burlington House Cartoon (after an English art collection that once owned it), is a magnificent work that some art critics and historians prefer over the later painting Leonardo did of the same subject.

# HOW TO PAINT A BATTLE SCENE

In his notebooks, Leonardo penned a long description of how one should properly paint a large battle scene, advice that modern scholars think he planned
to employ in his now lost artwork The Battle of Anghiari. He said in part:

The conquerors you will make rushing onwards with their hair and other
light things flying on the wind, with their brows bent down, and with the
opposite limbs thrust forward. . . . And if you make any one fallen, you must
show the place where he has slipped and been dragged along the dust into
blood-stained mire; and in the half-liquid earth around show the print of the
tramping of men and horses who have passed that way. Make also a horse
dragging the dead body of his master, and leaving behind him, in the dust
and mud, the track where the body was dragged along. You must make the
conquered and beaten pale, their brows raised and knit, and the skin above
their brows furrowed with pain, the sides of the nose with wrinkles going in
an arch from the nostrils to the eyes, and make the nostrils drawn up . . . and
the lips arched upwards and discovering the upper teeth; and the teeth apart
as with crying out and lamentation. . . . Others represent shouting with their
mouths open, and running away. You must scatter arms of all sorts among
the feet of the combatants, as broken shields, lances, broken swords and
other such objects. And you must make the dead partly or entirely covered
with dust, which is changed into crimson mire where it has mingled with the
flowing blood.

Leonardo da Vinci. *The Notebooks of
Leonardo da Vinci*. Translated by Jean Paul
Richter. Project Gutenberg. www.gutenberg
.org/cache/epub/5000/pg 5000.html.

*A surviving remnant of
Leonardo's The Battle of
Anghiari was painted from
his preliminary drawings.
The original was destroyed in
a fire.*

That later work, which shows Mary and the others in different poses from the ones in the earlier version, was completed sometime between 1507 and 1513. Even if it is does not measure up to Leonardo's first conception of the grouping, everyone agrees that it is a great painting in its own right. "St. Anne smiles tenderly upon her daughter, the Virgin Mary, who is sitting upon her lap," Elke Linda Buchholz writes. In turn, Mary

> bends down with a hint of refrained anxiety toward her son Jesus, who is playing with a lamb. This scene foreshadows his future role as the crucified Lamb of God. Leonardo has composed here a complicated group of people who seem to be in motion, and yet remain closely intertwined. By arranging this composition in the classical form of a pyramid, he lent the picture tranquility [and] compactness. The wide, rocky landscape with mountains disappearing behind the blue fog reflect Leonardo's close observation of nature.[36]

During the long period in which Leonardo worked on the different versions of *The Virgin and Child with St. Anne*, he also devoted time to various stages of other painting projects. One of the biggest was *The Battle of Anghiari*, a commission intended to grace an entire inner wall of Florence's Council Hall. (Florentines still celebrated Anghiari, fought in 1440, in which they defeated the forces of their arch rival, Milan.) The mural was intended to face a similar painting—the *Battle of Cascina*, by Leonardo's younger rival, the great Michelangelo—commissioned for the opposite wall.

Unfortunately for Leonardo, his countrymen, and posterity, the painting was never completed. Moreover, the parts that he did finish did not survive. Not long after he began work, a particularly harsh storm struck Florence, bringing with it extreme humidity, which kept the paint from drying. When Leonardo and his assistants tried to force-dry it using a fire, most of the existing paint melted off the wall, and in a fit of anger and despair, the artist gave up on the project.

Nevertheless, several of Leonardo's preparatory drawings for the painting have survived, as have drawings and paintings by other artists based on the images on the wall before they were destroyed. These indicate that if *The Battle of Anghiari* had come to fruition, it would have been an artistic masterpiece of epic proportions. Some idea of the awesome concepts Leonardo had in mind for it can be seen in a long passage in his notebooks in which he explains how to paint a battle scene. A small excerpt reads:

> You must represent the smoke of artillery mingling in the air with the dust and tossed up by the movement of horses and the combatants. . . . The higher the smoke mixed with the dust-laden air rises towards a certain level, the more it will look like a dark cloud; and . . . will assume a bluish tinge. . . . If you introduce horses galloping outside the crowd, make the little clouds of dust distant from each other in proportion to the strides made by the horses. [Also] the air must be full of arrows in every direction, some shooting upwards, some falling, some flying level.[37]

# The Image of Perfect Beauty

In 1503, the same year that Leonardo both began and gave up on the great battle painting, he also started work on a picture that was destined for true immortality. Entire volumes have been written about this one-of-a-kind artwork—the *Mona Lisa*. One of the foremost experts on the work cuts through the clutter and introduces it simply and definitively as "without doubt the most famous work in the entire forty-thousand-year history of the visual arts."[38]

Art historians agree that Leonardo finished the painting in 1507, after about four years of on-and-off work. However, they still *dis*agree about the identities of both the person who commissioned it and the individual portrayed in it. Theories about the subject of the painting range from various Spanish and Italian noblewomen to a man wearing women's clothes. The

Over the years, a number of people, both experts and laypeople, have noticed and remarked about the fact that the woman in Leonardo's Mona Lisa has no eyebrows. Noted art historian Robert Cumming addresses this point, saying:

The most likely explanation for [the lady's lack of eyebrows] is that Leonardo did put in eyebrows as a final touch onto the dry paint of the face, but the first time it was cleaned (perhaps in the seventeenth century), the restorer used the wrong solvent [cleaning fluid] and the eyebrows dissolved and were removed forever. It serves as a warning of how careful restorers must be.

Robert Cumming. *Annotated Art.* London: Dorling Kindersley, 1995, p. 26.

Leonardo's famous Mona Lisa *has no eyebrows. It is thought that a restorer's inadvertent use of the wrong solvent made them disappear.*

best guess—that is, the theory supported by the largest percentage of scholars—is that the person in the painting was Mona Lisa Gherardini. She was the wife of a wealthy Italian silk merchant, who, according to this view, commissioned Leonardo to do the portrait.

If this scenario is correct, the merchant never took possession of the work he had paid for. The *Mona Lisa* remained in Leonardo's possession for the rest of his life, apparently because he had an emotional attachment to it and refused to part with it. As art expert Robert Cumming puts it, "It is likely that the painting began as a portrait of a nobleman's wife but became something much more—the image of Leonardo's idea of perfect beauty."[39]

Most people who have seen the painting can sympathize with this view. There is general agreement among art lovers that, aside from Leonardo's technical mastery, the picture has a hard-to-define, compelling, and mysterious quality. This was well-articulated not long after the artist's death by Vasari, who said:

> In this head, whoever wished to see how closely art could imitate nature, was able to comprehend it with ease. . . . The eyes [have a] luster and watery sheen which are always seen in life, and around them [are] all those rosy and pearly tints, as well as the lashes, which cannot be represented without the greatest subtlety. . . . The nose, with its beautiful nostrils, rosy and tender, [appears] to be alive. The mouth, with its opening, and with its ends united by the red of the lips to the flesh-tints of the face, [seem], in truth, to be not colors but flesh. In the pit of the throat, if one gaze[s] upon it intently, [can] be seen the beating of the pulse. And, indeed, in this work of Leonardo's there [is] a smile so pleasing, that it [is] a thing more divine than human to behold.[40]

This conviction that the *Mona Lisa* possesses special qualities that appeal to the heart and emotions did not dim over the centuries. The eminent nineteenth-century English art critic Walter Pater wrote, "She is older than the rocks among

*Saint John the Baptist* was created sometime between 1501 and 1513. Saint John was one of Leonardo's favorite subjects, and he painted him several times.

which she sits. Like the vampire, she has been dead many times, and learned the secrets of the grave; and has been [a] diver in deep seas [of the human imagination]."[41]

Art experts agree that at least part of this mysterious and strangely alluring quality of the painting stems from the incredibly inventive, cleverly unnatural way that Leonardo used light in it. As Stefan Klein points out, it is

> remarkable how the light pours over Mona Lisa's body and plays with her fingers, each of which is finely shaded like a miniature sculpture. The hands project far forward to counterbalance the landscape in the distance, which augments [enhances] the painting's sense of depth. . . . Most importantly, the illumination makes Mona Lisa appear both animated and mysterious. The distribution of light and shadow foils any attempt to construe [figure out] her frame of mind. Obviously Leonardo calculated the brightness of each and every square inch of his painting to achieve a particular effect. Nevertheless, no detail seems contrived or calculated. The light that falls on the young woman appears quite natural. . . . But a closer look reveals that something is not quite right. The woman is sitting on a [balcony]. Therefore the illumination would have to come primarily from the open side of the balcony toward the landscape, so we ought to be seeing Mona Lisa *against* the light. But in Leonardo's painting, she is illuminated from the front upper left corner. . . . Leonardo, however, used the laws of optics to such perfect effect that the illusion is not conspicuous, [and] we simply accept that the young woman looks more real than reality itself. Leonardo did not paint this picture in accordance with reality. He created a new one—a virtual reality.[42]

# The Savior Rediscovered

The *Mona Lisa* was one of the paintings that the visiting cardinal's assistant, Antonio de Beatis, saw in the aged Leonardo's studio in France in 1517. By that time the artist had produced

This unknown artist's version of *Leda and the Swan* was taken from Leonardo's cartoons.

several more paintings or detailed cartoons for paintings, all begun between 1501 and 1513. Among them were *St. John the Baptist*, a depiction of one of Leonardo's favorite characters, this time seen as an adult; *Leda and the Swan*, the cartoon for a picture of a famous character from Greek mythology; and the *Madonna of the Yarnwinder*, a small painting of Mary and Jesus that most art authorities presume has been lost.

Another of Leonardo's paintings from this period was also long thought lost. Evidence indicates that in 1506 France's King Louis XII commissioned the artist to create a portrait of Jesus Christ, and supposedly the work, titled *Salvator Mundi* ("Savior of the World"), was completed in 1513. Leonardo had it in his possession, but after his passing in 1519, the painting's trail of ownership became unclear. Although several copies of the work were painted later by his assistants or other well-known artists, the whereabouts of the original remained unknown.

In 2005, however, one of those copies, long assumed to have been created by one of Leonardo's apprentices, was discovered to be the real thing. The reason that its true identity had not been guessed earlier was that it had been over-painted at least once by an artist whose talent was clearly inferior to the master's. After art experts had removed the outer layer of paint, it took them less than a day to authenticate the work as Leonardo's glorious original. The excited Pietro Marani, a Milan-based world-renowned expert on Leonardo, said in part, "The blues and the reds in the painting are very similar to those of Da Vinci's *Last Supper* and the pigment is also very similar to his *Virgin on the Rocks* painting."[43]

The *Salvator Mundi* shows a calm and relaxed Jesus staring out at the viewer, with his right hand raised as if to give a blessing. His left hand holds a crystalline globe that appears to represent Earth or the entire universe. The painting's powerful portrayal of the human face, rich colors, and technical mastery all combine to form an image no less exquisite and moving as that of the *Mona Lisa*. Both pictures live on to testify to the unarguable artistic genius of the man who created them.

# Dabbling in Architecture and Sculpture

Leonardo da Vinci is best known to the modern world for his paintings. But he was gifted in other artistic disciplines, including architecture and sculpture. For various logistical, or practical, reasons, a majority of them beyond his control, most of his proposed architectural and sculptural projects never became reality. Yet his many preliminary drawings, plus descriptions of the projects surviving in his notes or letters by others, provide valuable information about them. Moreover, some of this evidence, especially relating to the large sculptures, gives a fairly good idea of what these artworks would have looked like. In addition, for his proposed large-scale sculptures, Leonardo designed a new metal-casting process that strongly influenced all later European sculptors.

## Adventures in Architecture

Leonardo's keen interest in architecture is obvious from the numerous references to that combination of art and science in his writings. He was apparently particularly fascinated with designing cathedrals, and his notes and drawings are alive with renditions of church interiors and exteriors, too, including large domes atop the roofs. It must have been thrilling for him, therefore, when he heard that Milan's government wanted to add a new *tiburio*, or domed tower, on the roof of the city's main cathedral. A competition to select the architect for this project was announced in 1487. After conceiving a design, Leonardo hired a carpenter named Bernardo di Abbiate to construct a large, detailed model of his proposed addition.

When presenting his design for the dome, Leonardo included a formal cover letter, which has survived. In it, among other things, he compared the work of an architect to that of a doctor, saying, "You know that medicines, when they are properly used, restore health to invalids, and that he who knows [such medicines] thoroughly . . . will be a more effective healer than any other. This too is what the sick cathedral needs—it needs a doctor-architect, who understands the nature of the building, and the laws upon which correct construction is based."[44]

The contest attracted a number of excellent architects, so Leonardo faced stiff competition. In the end he was likely disappointed at not winning, yet he may have found some consolation in the fact that no one actually emerged the sole victor. "The whole affair was quite complicated," Serge Bramly points out.

> On May 31, [1490], the architects [including Leonardo] met to try to devise a compromise. They discussed it at length without managing to agree. . . . Finally, all the competitors met for one last discussion . . . in front of Lodovico himself. . . . The final design was [an] amalgam [combination] of all the entries submitted. It is possible that Francesco di Giorgio . . . worked out the final design in conversation with Leonardo.[45]

Other architectural projects that Leonardo partially or fully designed but that never actually broke ground include a summer villa for an Italian nobleman, designed in 1501. He planned for it to have large, airy rooms that opened onto elegant porches and garden walkways. Some evidence suggests that he also intended to erect a replica of a Roman temple to the goddess Venus and a human-made lake on the villa's grounds. He wrote in his proposal:

You will make steps on four sides, leading up to a naturally formed meadow on the summit of a rock. The rock will be hollowed out and supported at the front with pillars, and beneath it a huge [porch] where water flows into various basins . . . and let the water in these be continually running over. And facing this [porch], towards the north, let there be a lake, and in the middle of it a little island with a thick shady wood.[46]

Leonardo's preliminary sketches for a domed structure for a church in Milan, Italy.

# Why Walls Crack

*Leonardo made a number of entries about one of his passions, architecture, in his notebooks. In this passage, sounding much like a modern scientist, he theorizes about what causes instability and, eventually, cracks in a building.*

The walls give way in cracks, some of which are more or less vertical and others are oblique [at an angle]. The cracks which are in a vertical direction are caused by the joining of new walls, with old walls, whether straight or with indentations fitting on to those of the old wall; for, as these indentations cannot bear the too great weight of the wall added on to them, it is inevitable that they should break, and give way to the settling of the new wall. . . . And observe, that the walls should always be built first and then faced with the stones intended to face them. For, if you do not proceed thus, since the wall settles more than the stone facing, the projections left on the sides of the wall must inevitably give way.

Leonardo da Vinci. *The Notebooks of Leonardo da Vinci.* Translated by Jean Paul Richter. Project Gutenberg. www.gutenberg.org/cache/epub/5000/pg5000.html.

Still another architectural adventure that never came to fruition, this one conceived for Duke Lodovico, was an entire city that the designer intended to be as up-to-date and practical as possible. The ultimate problem was that building this metropolis would have required tearing down most of existing Milan. Needless to say, the duke saw the political and social obstacles in the way of such a grandiose scheme and vetoed it.

Later, in 1517, Leonardo began work on designs for a new palace complex for the French king. This project, like the others, never got off the ground. However, architectural historians think the plans Leonardo drew up for the palace were so impressive that they strongly influenced the next generation of French architects. In this way some of the royal buildings erected in France in the following few centuries likely owed part of their shape and charm to a brilliant Italian artist who had once briefly visited the country.

# The Early Sculptures

It is unknown what Leonardo thought about the intrinsic merits of architecture. But he was very clear about how he felt about sculpture. In an often-cited passage from his notebooks, he explained why sculpture was inferior to painting, saying in part:

> I myself, having exercised myself no less in sculpture than in painting and doing both one and the other in the same degree, it seems to me that I can . . . pronounce an opinion as to which of the two is of the greatest merit and difficulty and perfection. . . . If you will have me only speak of painting on panel [wood], I am content to pronounce between it and sculpture. Saying that painting is the more beautiful and the more imaginative and the more copious [plentiful], while sculpture is the more durable but it has nothing else. Sculpture shows with little labor what in painting appears a miraculous thing to do. . . . In fact, painting is adorned with infinite possibilities which sculpture cannot command.[47]

In spite of his evident intellectual disdain for sculpture, Leonardo was not above fashioning various objects in that three-dimensional art. In fact, he involved himself in a number of sculptural projects throughout most of this adult career as an artist. As in his architectural pursuits, few of the sculptures he designed ever became finished products. Yet his sketches and the surviving comments of his contemporaries reveal that he had the potential to become one of the finest sculptors of the Renaissance.

Leonardo crafted his first sculptures during his long apprenticeship to Verrocchio. In his biography of Leonardo, Vasari mentions that he "worked in sculpture" in his master's studio, "making in his youth, in clay, some heads of women that are smiling, of which plaster casts are still taken, and likewise some heads of boys which appeared to have issued from the hand of a master."[48] Another sculpted piece attributed to the young Leonardo is a 13-inch-tall (33cm) terra-cotta (baked clay) head generally referred to as the *Youthful Christ*. A later owner of the head, Giovanni Paolo Lamazzo, wrote, "I have also a little terracotta head of Christ when he was a boy, sculpted by Leonardo Vinci's own hand, in which one sees the simplicity and purity of the boy, together with a certain something which shows wisdom, intellect, and majesty. He [the

One of Leonardo's early sculptures is the *Youthful Christ*.

Long considered to be the work of Verrocchio, the sculpture *Bust of a Woman with Flowers* is now thought to have been done by the young Leonardo.

sculpted Christ] has an air that may be tenderness of youth but which seems also old and wise."[49]

Not only do many scholars think that Verrocchio used the youthful Leonardo as the model for his statue of David, some also recently proposed that that same young apprentice was the true author of another sculpture that was long assumed to be by Verrocchio himself. The piece in question is the *Bust of a Woman with Flowers*. "This work is significant for being the first bust in Renaissance art which displayed the hands," Maxine Annabell remarks. It was probably "done between 1475–1480."[50]

Among the other sculptures that Leonardo evidently did while working in Verrocchio's studio are two terra-cotta angels now on display in the Louvre. A number of modern experts think they are Leonardo's because of their close resemblance to the angel he painted in Verrocchio's *Baptism of Christ*. Another similar sculpted angel, also attributed to Leonardo, was found in modern times in a church in the hilltop village of San Gennaro, in northern Italy. Noted novelist and researcher Charles Nicholl describes it as "a beautiful piece, alert and full of movement." He adds: "The angel's right arm is an unmistakable echo of the *Annunciation* angel [attributed to Leonardo], and the long curling hair is a Leonardo trademark."[51] Nicholl thinks that Leonardo sculpted the angel in 1477 while passing through the region in which the village is located, perhaps to earn some extra money for his personal expenses. If this is true, the piece has probably been in the little church ever since, long unbeknownst to the art world.

# The Great Horse

For Leonardo, these small, youthful sculptures were completely overshadowed by an enormous project that came to his attention in 1483. It was a gigantic bronze equestrian statue that Duke Lodovico commissioned, which was to show his father, Francesco Sforza, atop a magnificent horse. Various modern estimates have been made of the original specs for the monument, which are somewhat unclear. One estimate suggests that the finished sculpture would have stood 26 feet (8m) high and weighed 158,000 pounds (71,574kg), or 79 tons (71.7t). That would have made it more than twice as high and many times as massive as any other equestrian sculpture that then existed.

Leonardo was eager to do the great statue, which came to be called *Il Cavallo*, meaning "the horse." He told Duke Lodovico, "The bronze horse . . . is to be the immortal glory and eternal honor of the prince, your father, of happy memory, and of the illustrious house of Sforza."[52] Wanting to do a good job on the project, Leonardo as usual put in a large amount of preparation, including many drawings and notes. Among these writings are some quick, often disconnected entries to his notebooks meant to record some of his scattered thoughts about molding such a bulky equestrian statue. "Make the horse on legs of iron, strong and well set on a good foundation," he began.

> Draw upon the horse, when finished, all the pieces of the mold with which you wish to cover the horse, and in laying on the clay cut it in every piece, so that when the mold is finished you can take it off, and then re-compose it in its former position. . . . The clay should be mixed with sand. Take wax, to return [what is not used] and to pay for what is used. Dry it in layers. Make the outside mold of plaster, to save time in drying and the expense in wood. . . . Make terracotta. And this mold can be made in one day. Half a boat load of plaster will serve you. Good. Dam it up again with glue and clay, or white of egg, and bricks and rubbish.[53]

The main problem that Leonardo faced in approaching the statue was not his lack of vision and ingenuity. Of those qualities he possessed more than enough. The difficulty was in the casting, for no one had ever before attempted to cast such a large and immensely heavy mass of bronze. Indeed, nearly every artist in Milan and other Italian cities thought it was impossible, among them even the great sculptor Michelangelo. He and Leonardo did not get along, and the story of one of their confrontations has survived. In it, they supposedly passed each other on the street several years later, and the younger man, Michelangelo, shouted, "You are the one who made a design for a horse to be cast in bronze, and you couldn't cast it!" Turning on his heel, he started to storm away, but then spun around and yelled, "And those Milanese idiots believed in you?"[54]

It was said that Leonardo did not try to defend himself in that encounter. It was perfectly true that he could not cast the horse using the prevailing methods of the time. Yet that did not stop him from inventing a completely new technique—sectional molding, or piece molding. In that complex process, several negative (or female) and positive (or male) molds are made from a clay model, and liquid bronze is poured into a matrix, or open space, that forms between the final negative and positive molds. Italian art expert Maria Vittoria Brugnoli briefly comments on the advantages of this revolutionary approach.

One of Leonardo's early sketches for his equestrian statue of Francesco Sforza, Duke Lodovico's father. It was to be twice as large as any other equestrian statue of the time, but the sculpture was never completed.

In the ingenious method Leonardo invented to cast large bronze objects, he first created a clay model, from which he made an outer female, or negative, mold of plaster. Next he lined the female mold with wax or potter's clay. From that, he fashioned a male, or positive, mold of clay. Then he took it all apart and rebaked the male mold, after which he placed it back inside the female mold, making sure to remove the wax or clay in the process. In the empty space Leonardo had created, he cast some wax in order to make a counter-model of the original. He then made a new clay female mold and heated it to make the wax melt and dribble out. Finally, he refitted the new female mold onto the male one and poured bronze into the cavity created by the missing wax.

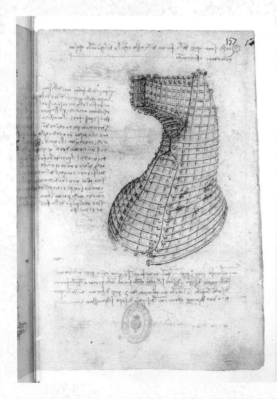

*Leonardo's sketch of a model for the casting of his Gian Giacomo Trivulzio equestrian statue. The artist invented new techniques for sectional bronze castings of large sculptures.*

The greatest achievement of Leonardo's new system of sectional molding was that a hollow plaster impression was obtained in which it would be possible to cast wax to obtain a counter-model [wax copy] of the original. The artist could check this counter-model for deficiencies that might have occurred in the first impression, correct them, and trim the counter-model until maximum perfection in the image to be translated into bronze had been achieved. The molding process was thus no longer a matter of high-level manual labor, but rather a creative work that demanded the presence and intervention [direct involvement] of the artist.[55]

# A Last Chance Lost

In the mid-1490s, while Leonardo was waiting for Duke Lodovico to collect enough bronze to cast the huge statue, the artist found that his creation of the large clay model of the horse had already made him famous throughout Italy. The people of Milan were thrilled with and proud of the clay giant. Leonardo also kept himself busy with designs for four bigger-than-normal furnaces that would be needed to do the casting, as well as with his paintings, scientific researches, and drawings.

The giant metal horse was not destined to be cast, however. By the time that most of the bronze had been gathered, the French were threatening northern Italy, and Lodovico ordered the metal to be used for making cannons. The massive clay model was sitting in a Milan courtyard when the French entered the city in 1499. French archers proceeded to use it for target practice, after which the weather steadily reduced it to a formless mound of moldy clay. In this way the seemingly countless hours Leonardo had put into the project over several years came to nothing.

What at first appeared to be another chance to create a large, lasting equestrian monument materialized in 1511, when Leonardo was almost sixty. Gian Giacomo Trivulzio, a Milanese military officer in service to the French, asked the

Leonardo's sketch of a horse to be used in an equestrian sculpture of Gian Giacomo Trivulzio. Although the sculpture was not completed, drawings and studies have been preserved.

# PAINTING SUPERIOR TO SCULPTURE?

*In his notebooks Leonardo compared the arts of painting and sculpture and told why he felt that painting was the superior of the two.*

ℐn the first place, sculpture requires a certain light, that is from above, [whereas] a picture carries everywhere with it its own light and shade. Thus sculpture owes its importance to light and shade, and the sculptor is aided in this by the nature of the relief which is inherent in it, while the painter whose art expresses the accidental aspects of nature, places his effects in the spots where nature must necessarily produce them. The sculptor cannot diversify his work by the various natural colors of objects. Painting is not defective in any particular. The sculptor, when he uses perspective, cannot make it in any way appear true. [The perspective] of the painter can appear like a hundred miles beyond the picture itself. [Sculptors'] works have no aerial perspective whatever, they cannot represent transparent bodies, they cannot represent luminous bodies, nor reflected lights, nor lustrous bodies—as mirrors and the like polished surfaces, nor mists, nor dark skies, nor an infinite number of things [that a painting can easily depict].

Leonardo da Vinci. *The Notebooks of Leonardo da Vinci*. Translated by Jean Paul Richter. Project Gutenberg. www.gutenberg.org/cache/epub/5000/pg5000.html.

aging artist to sculpt a large bronze horse for the tomb in which Trivulzio would one day be buried. Leonardo's surviving drawings of the statue show that the horse and rider would have assumed a dramatic, exciting pose. Also, the pedestal on which the horse was to stand would have been beautifully decorated with pillars and elaborate carvings.

However, once more fate seemed to intervene to ruin his plans. In 1512 a combined army of Swiss, Spaniards, and others drove the French, and Trivulzio with them, out of Milan. Leonardo had lost both his new patron and his last chance for creating a major sculptural legacy. Perhaps if he had known that many centuries later even his mere sketches for the equestrian statues would be viewed as priceless art treasures, he might have been less upset about the unfinished horses.

# Recording Visual Reality: The Drawings

When examining Leonardo's oeuvre, or total output, as an artist, it is immediately apparent that his drawings make up a substantial and important portion of it. Indeed, art historians estimate that he did upward of twenty-one hundred drawings in all, a bit more than six hundred of which have survived. To make them, he employed several different instruments, including black and red chalk, pen and ink, silverpoint (a silver wire or sharpened silver rod), brushes, and others. In fact, it seems likely that he originated the use of sharpened pieces of red chalk for drawing. Moreover, he may also have invented the related use of pastels (multicolored chalks), which first appeared in the works of his apprentices.

## A Wide Range of Subjects

The subjects of Leonardo's drawings cover almost the entire range of human knowledge that existed in his time. On the one hand, some of his sketches were preliminary studies for his paintings and sculptures. Preparatory drawings for the *Adoration of the Magi*, *The Madonna of the Rocks*, *Madonna of the Yarnwinder*, the great bronze horse for Duke Lodovico, and other major works, both finished and unfinished, have survived.

Leonardo's sketch of his world-renowned *Vitruvian Man* displays the ideal proportions of the human form. Many of his drawings explore the beauty of the human body.

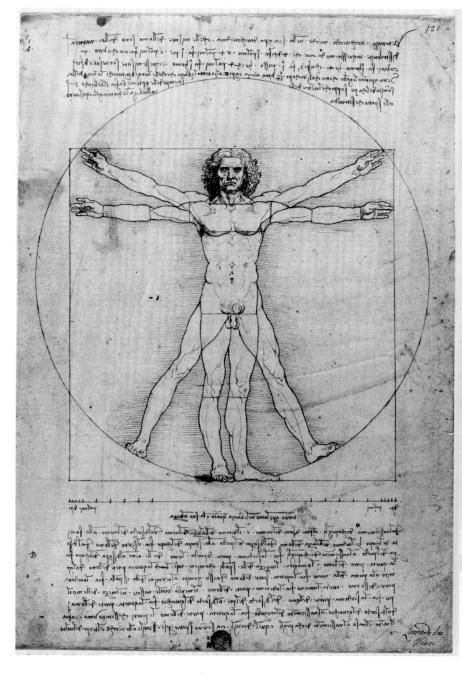

On the other hand, many of Leonardo's drawings were independent studies in themselves. Many of these explore the beauty of the human form, while others capture the complexity of animals; trees, mountains, running water, and other natural forms; and architectural and mechanical objects, including the artist's own ingenious inventions. Overall, Jack Wasserman points out, these drawings were Leonardo's way of creating "records of visual reality," so that he could better understand "animate [living] and inanimate [nonliving] nature, its form, structure, movement, dynamics, individual character, and force—and where [humans were] concerned, expression."[56]

Whether they were intended as preliminary studies for artworks or as independent studies of the natural world, Leonardo's drawings were almost always extremely detailed and thorough. Therein lies the great contradiction in his mind, between art and life. In his numerous scientific studies and inventions, he rarely followed up on and made physical, workable versions of the things he drew as an artist. As Robert Wallace explains:

> The meticulousness [exactness] of his drawings indicates . . . that he harbored at least the thought of putting his ideas into practice. But he never did. Leonardo always seemed to go on to other things before he took the final step of bringing his projects to concrete, functioning reality. His notes and drawings remained his own secret. He did not allow them to be examined, tested, or put to use.[57]

This is why Leonardo was always more of an artist than a scientist. Art is subjective and can be evaluated and judged privately by anyone. Conversely, science must be reviewed and evaluated in the open, in the practical world. The retiring, solitary Leonardo dealt with that world only when he had to, and in so doing barred himself from becoming a formal, accomplished scientist. For him, science remained a mostly underdeveloped sector of the private artistic province of his drawings.

# Portraying Humanity

Among the most striking of Leonardo's surviving drawings are his many portraits of men and women of varying ages. Several are studies of the face of the Virgin Mary, a character he painted frequently. He typically depicted her with soft, attractive features and a modest smile. Other portraits are of people Leonardo knew—for instance, a black chalk rendering from 1500 showing Isabella D'Este, wife of the ruler of the Italian city of Mantua.

There are also a number of self-portraits among Leonardo's drawings, of which one, known as the Turin drawing, is particularly famous and familiar to most people. It dates from 1512, when he was sixty. Done in red chalk, probably shortly before he departed Milan for Rome, it shows him balding in front and wearing a thick white beard. Serge Bramly writes:

> Leonardo manages to create a soft image without losing any precision of line or form. Every hair is there.... [By this time] his health was failing, age and long study had weakened his eyes [and] under the light mustache, the shrunken upper lip reveals that his teeth had gone.... In this portrait, there would be no self-deception. Rather, he was studying himself scientifically, catching himself unawares, so to speak. He scrutinized the worn features of the old man he had become, as if they were those of a stranger. The mysterious power of the drawing may derive from this. Leonardo is summing up his life with a crayon.[58]

Not long before Leonardo captured himself in the Turin drawing, his faithful assistant Francesco Melzi initiated a portrait of his master. Leonardo seems to have finished it or touched it up. It has a somewhat similar appearance to the Turin drawing, showing a long, thick beard, except that in this one he is posed in profile. Also, the young shepherd wearing a cloak in the far-right side of the cartoon for the *Adoration of the Magi* is thought to be an early attempt by Leonardo to capture his own likeness.

In addition, the face of the famous *Vitruvian Man*, a Leonardo drawing dating from circa 1490, may be based on that of its creator. This sketch, often used in modern books, posters, and TV programs as a trademark for Leonardo, shows a naked man's body, with arms outstretched, superimposed on

Leonardo's self-portrait dates from 1512, when he was sixty years old.

that of another man, both standing within a large circle. It was intended to show the geometric ratios of the human body. "The stern-looking man in the circle seems to be *someone*," Charles Nicholl speculates, rather than a "cipher," or generic individual. That someone has "penetrating, deeply shadowed eyes, and a thick mane of curly hair." At the least, "there are *elements* of self-portraiture in the Vitruvian Man." Indeed, "this figure that represents natural harmonies also represents the man uniquely capable of understanding them—the artist-anatomist-architect Leonardo da Vinci."[59]

# From Hideous to Sublime

In addition to studies of people that Leonardo viewed as "normal," he produced numerous drawings of oddly shaped, exotic-looking individuals. Collectively, they are often referred to as "grotesques." The people in question most often had overly large noses, chins, or other features; few or no teeth; and frequently, menacing demeanors or highly unusual personalities.

The most famous example is a large drawing Leonardo did in the early 1490s. It displays five repulsive-looking characters, all positioned close to one another. The central figure, versions of which appear in many of Leonardo's sketches, has a huge hooked nose and wears a crown of oak leaves, as if he is pretending to be some sort of emperor. Of the four faces surrounding him, one is in the midst of a wild laugh or scream. The second is seemingly lost in thought; the third displays a demonic grin complete with rotten teeth; and the fourth has a horribly protruding lower lip and puffy jowls. If the artist had some specific meaning or statement in mind when he did the drawing, no one has yet been able to decipher it.

As if deftly moving from the hideous to the sublime, Leonardo also put enormous amounts of time and energy into reproducing the intricate beauty of the bones, muscles, and organs of the human body. His numerous anatomical drawings were the end result of long hours spent dissecting corpses. Much of this work was done in the medical school of the University of Pavia, a town lying 22 miles (35km) south of Milan.

*In his notebooks, Leonardo addressed various aspects of the art of drawing. In this passage, he points out a common pitfall for an artist to avoid in selecting human faces to draw.*

**L**ook about you and take the best parts of many beautiful faces, of which the beauty is confirmed rather by public fame than by your own judgment. For you might be mistaken and choose faces which have some resemblance to your own. For it would seem that such resemblances often please us. And if you should be ugly, you would select faces that were not beautiful and you would then make ugly faces, as many painters do. For often a master's work resembles himself. So select beauties as I tell you, and fix them in your mind.

Leonardo da Vinci. *The Notebooks of Leonardo da Vinci.* Translated by Jean Paul Richter. Project Gutenberg. www.gutenberg.org/cache/epub/5000/pg5000.html.

*Among his other talents, Leonardo also drew caricatures; his renderings of a man and two women are shown here. The style features comical or grotesque exaggerations of physical characteristics.*

Leonardo intended eventually to collect all of the anatomical drawings and publish them as a major treatise on anatomy. Had he done so, one expert points out, "he would have transformed the study of human anatomy in Europe."[60] Regrettably for him and posterity, however, the aging artist never managed

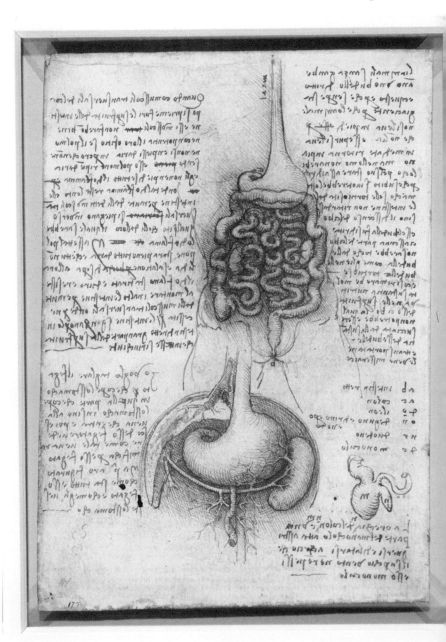

Leonardo's drawings of the human stomach and intestines. His notably accurate anatomical drawings are derived from the long hours he spent dissecting corpses.

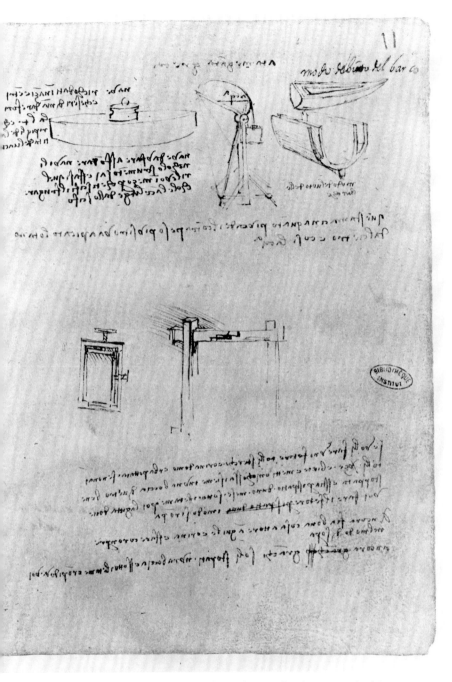

to find the time to complete this task. As a result, his anatomical drawings ended up buried amidst piles of writings and sketches, most of which were not made public or thoroughly examined by scholars until modern times.

These truly masterful anatomical drawings present both exterior and interior views of nearly every part of the human body. Moreover, the level of detail and accuracy is often extraordinary, making them examples of both great art and great science. From their comprehensive study of these sketches, scholars Martin Clayton and Ron Philo point out one page that includes muscles of the arm, shoulder, hand, and face.

> Leonardo fits a remarkable amount of information onto this page. . . . These studies of the facial muscles are astonishingly accurate. The drawing to the left [of the page] depicts the superficial [outer] muscles, notoriously difficult to dissect as they may originate and/or insert into the deep surface of the skin. In the drawing at center, some of the superficial muscles have been removed to reveal the deep structures. Though Leonardo did not distinguish formally between the . . . muscles of facial expression and the primary muscles of mastication [chewing], he did attempt to identify the function of each. [He also drew] the complex of muscles that raise the upper lip [and] in a note [he] reminds himself to see if this is the same muscle that raises the [nostrils] of the horse, an action that he had examined in his studies for the Battle of Anghiari five years earlier.[61]

# Military Facilities and Machines

In addition to his representations of human faces and bodies, Leonardo turned out reams of drawings of forts, fortifications, and other defensive facilities, as well as weapons of war. These were mostly done during the years he worked as an engineer or architect for Duke Lodovico and Cesare Borgia. Typical of the fortifications are those designed around 1502 for Borgia, who had recently taken over the charming port city of Piombino, on Italy's northwestern coast. Leonardo's sketches indicate that he planned four main projects for the town. One was to dig a trench

1,260 feet (384m) long from the citadel, or main fort, to a nearby peninsula. Defenders would have been able to hide in the trench and direct their fire against invaders landing in boats and trying to attack the citadel. The second proposed project was a tunnel 590 feet (180m) long, running from the citadel to the town gate. This was to provide an escape route, if necessary, for those defending the citadel. Third, Leonardo designed a new, larger tower for the citadel, and fourth, he planned to level a nearby hill so that the defenders could achieve a more effective line of fire against an approaching enemy.

Two years before, when visiting Venice on Italy's opposite coast, Leonardo had designed some fortifications and some offensive weapons, too, for the local leaders. At the time, Venice was under threat from a Turkish land army and fleet. Leonardo drew a map and on one side of it sketched his plan to stop the invading land troops by flooding the valley through which they planned to approach the city. To destroy the Turkish fleet, he designed diving suits and a small submarine. These, he showed, could be used to attack the enemy boats' hulls from below. "The submarine," Maxine Annabell explains, "was simply a shell with room enough for one person to sit inside. It was topped with a conning tower which had a lid and pre-dated the true submarine by over one hundred years. Leonardo [described] it as a 'ship to sink another ship.'"[62] (It is unknown whether the Venetians actually built and used any of these devices.)

Leonardo drew many other ingenious offensive weapons. One, designed for Duke Lodovico about a year after the artist's first arrival in Milan, consists of two lances attached to and protruding from a cavalryman's saddle. These were meant to supplement the rider's handheld lance, as shown in one of Leonardo's more fascinating sketches. "The tripling of the rider's lance power," scholar Bern Dibner writes, "must have appealed to Leonardo's penchant [fondness] for designs that multiplied a simple force."[63]

One of the most impressive weapons seen among Leonardo's drawings is a gigantic ballista, a form of artillery, or stone thrower, used by the ancient Greeks and Romans. In the

Leonardo designed many machines of war. Shown here is his drawing of a giant crossbow.

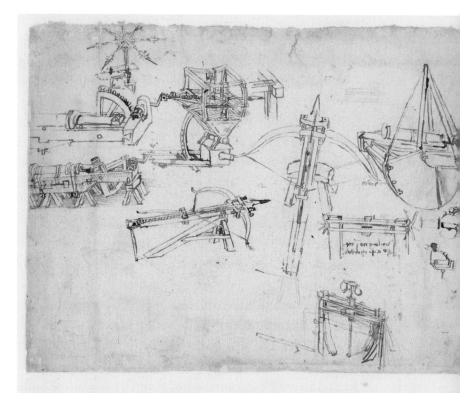

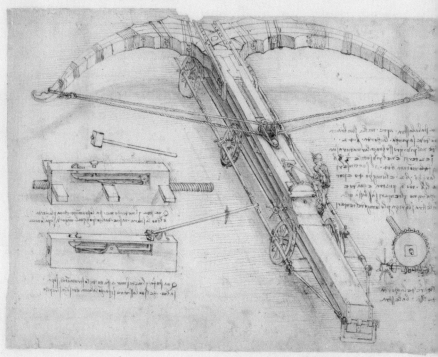

detailed sketch, the two large, bow-like arms are constructed in several sections, like a composite bow. Modern experts say that this arrangement would give them plenty of flexibility, so that the ropes attached to their ends could be pulled very far back, creating extra tension. Cradled at the junction of those ropes in the drawing is a huge stone missile. On the sketch's left side, the artist inserts close-ups of two alternate mechanisms for releasing the tension in the ropes and thereby launching the missile.

Leonardo's giant ballista was a larger, more inventive version of a much older weapon, so it was not a completely new idea. His design for what has been called a "machine-gun" crossbow *was* revolutionary, however. Dibner describes the device in his elaborate drawing, saying:

> Tension is given to the strings of each of four bows mounted on the inner periphery of a large treadwheel. The treadwheel is rotated on a horizontal axle by a team of men who walk on a circumference of outer treads and thereby provide continuous rotation for rapid fire. An archer hangs suspended in the mechanism's center. His task is to trigger each crossbow as it descends . . . [and shoot] through [a] slot in the structure.[64]

In a similar vein, Leonardo drew plans for a multiple-barreled light cannon that clearly anticipated the Gatling gun, an early machine gun invented in the 1800s. He also designed stubby mortars, or short-barreled cannons, that looked exactly like those used in the American Civil War in the 1860s. Indeed, one scholar asserts, even "a casual examination of some of Leonardo's sketches would indicate that his techniques were those of an artillerist of the mid-1800s. In some respects, he was ahead of even those days."[65]

# The Dream of Human Flight

Some of Leonardo's drawings show that he was definitely ahead of his time in his attempts to design a practical way for humans to fly like birds. Among his most famous sketches are studies of birds in flight and of people donning elaborate mechanical wings of his own design. The problem throughout most of the twenty-five years he devoted to the dream of human flight was that he was approaching the problem from the wrong angle. Leonardo long assumed that the only answer was to literally mimic birds—by the flapping of wings. Initially, he did not conceive that a human's arms simply cannot produce enough power to make this possible.

Eventually, however, the great artist-inventor began to catch on to the potential of using gliders for human flight. According to Stefan Klein:

> Leonardo started to realize, during his final years in Milan, that beating wings was insufficient for flight. Humans were simply too weak to rise into the sky on their own power. . . . He returned to studying nature [and] noticed that the larger the bird, the less frequently it flapped its wings. Now he saw a solution that made it possible to remain aloft for hours. . . . Leonardo had understood that in gliding the critical element is achieving the optimal shape of the wing. Only then can the wings transform the headwinds into lift.[66]

For reasons that remain uncertain, as he often did in his scientific studies and speculation, Leonardo did not follow up on his ideas for gliders. Despite some romantic tales that circulated after his death, as near as modern scholars can tell, he did not actually build a full-sized glider and either pilot it himself or have someone else do so. Nevertheless, his surviving sketches prove that he understood the potential of that approach to flight. Also, some of his other drawings show diverse flight-related inventions, including the parachute, the helicopter, and a device to measure wind speed. That he took the time to draw these things in detail is often seen as an indication that he believed humans would one day fly.

Conversely, as Serge Bramly points out, he made at least one statement that suggests he thought human flight was hopeless. "Because of their ambition," Leonardo said in the

*This passage from Leonardo's writings was written before he realized that humans do not have enough physical strength, especially in their arms, to flap artificial wings vigorously enough to achieve sustained flight. (He later changed his mind and began designing gliders.)*

*A*n object offers as much resistance to the air as the air does to the object. You may see that the beating of its wings against the air supports a heavy eagle in the highest and rarest atmosphere, close to the sphere of elemental fire [the part of the sky then thought to exist above Earth's atmosphere]. Again you may see the air in motion over the sea fill the swelling sails and drive heavily laden ships. From these instances, and the reasons given, a man with wings large enough and duly connected might learn to overcome the resistance of the air, and by conquering it, succeed in subjugating it and rising above it.

Leonardo da Vinci. *The Notebooks of Leonardo da Vinci.* Translated by Jean Paul Richter. Project Gutenberg. www.gutenberg.org/cache/epub/5000/pg5000.html.

*Leonardo spent a large amount of time studying the wings of birds. Based on his research, he designed this human-powered ornithopter, which was intended to fly by the flapping of its wings. He would later design gliders.*

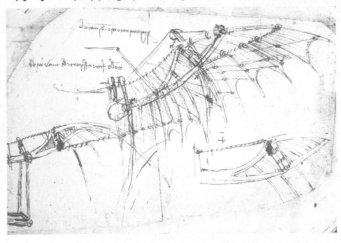

late 1490s, "some men will wish to rise to the sky. But the excessive weight of their limbs will hold them down."[67] Perhaps, as some experts speculate, he spoke these words in a bitter mood after conducting a never-documented flight test that ended in failure. Whatever motive he had for such a negative attitude, it appears to have been a passing phase. The fact is that a few years later he resumed creating drawings of ingenious devices intended to help people fly. One thing always remained true of Leonardo. This was that many of the beliefs, aspirations, and dreams that he never put in writing were plainly expressed in his many and wonderful drawings.

# 6

# Leonardo's Enduring Legacy

When Leonardo died in 1519, he left behind an enormous legacy, one that unfolded a little at a time and today continues to grow and amaze each new generation. As a painter alone, his influence has been extraordinarily far reaching. By early modern times his name had become a household word throughout the Western world, in part because he had created the most famous and beloved painting in history, the *Mona Lisa*. In addition, artists, art critics, and art historians in all the generations that succeeded him felt the impact of that picture and/or his entire output of paintings. Italian art historian Marco Rosci writes:

> From the nineteenth century to this day, no work of art has been subjected to such a weight of extravagant descriptive literature. . . . Nor has any [other] famous picture achieved such enormous popularity . . . as the result of mass-produced, low-priced, commercial reproductions. When the original painting was stolen in 1911 by an Italian mason (soon being found in Florence and restored to the Louvre), public reaction verged on hysteria. [The *Mona Lisa* also served] as a model for later generations of portrait painters [following Leonardo's demise].[68]

Like the great Italian Renaissance painter Raphael (shown here in a self-portrait), many artists of the time studied, copied, and learned from Leonardo's *Mona Lisa* and *The Last Supper*. Leonardo's influence on Renaissance art was considerable.

Among the first of those younger painters who held Leonardo and his paintings in awe and closely studied both was the great Italian Renaissance painter Raphael (1453–1520). The latter arrived in Florence in 1504 at the age of twenty-one and immediately fell under the spell of the older artist. To develop his abilities at portraiture, Raphael executed several drawings based on the *Mona Lisa*. "A good example," Roy McMullen says, "is a drawing that has been dated as early as 1504." The details of its composition "are all derivative," or copied from, the *Mona Lisa* "beyond any reasonable doubt."[69] Like Raphael, numerous later painters studied, copied, and/or learned from the *Mona Lisa*, *The Last Supper*, *The Virgin of the Rocks*, and other paintings by Leonardo containing human portraits.

# An Explorer of the World

Leonardo's artistic legacy contains much more than his influence as a painter, however. His vast collection of drawings was the outlet he used to express his many ideas about the world, life, science, and the pursuit of human progress. That last area—the potential progress and betterment of the human race and its society—is key to understanding the way Leonardo's mind worked and his approach to expressing himself in his art. The subjects of his paintings were rooted in the world of his own time. But large numbers of his drawings depict ideas and devices that belong to a world that did not yet exist and that he hoped to help shape. As one modern scholar puts it:

> His sketches offered a vision of a distant future in which people would understand the forces of nature and work with machines. [Of his collected drawings], turning a single page would transport [the viewer] to a very different, though no less fantastic world. Leonardo used chalk and pen to draw the inside of a human heart and a fetus growing in a womb. Other drawings showed aerial views of Italian landscapes and cities—the way we might see them from an airplane today. . . . [Because of such futuristic art] Leonardo is

now finally taken seriously not just as [a painter], but also as an explorer of our world. [In] the past, scholars who studied [him] were primarily art historians, [but] when heart surgeons, physicists, and engineers now look at these same projects . . . they are amazed at what they find.[70]

Indeed, even before the twentieth century, during which science took grand leaps forward, Leonardo's anatomical studies had a profound influence on doctors and the science of medicine. In 1773 noted English anatomist William Hunter

## "SEDUCED BY HIS GENIUS"

*Italian art historian Francesca Debolini here touches on some of the later European artists who felt Leonardo's influence.*

In both theory and practice, Leonardo's artistic influence in 16th- and 17th-century Europe, notably France, Spain, Flanders, and Germany, was immense. Copies, variants, and engravings demonstrate how easily his range of compositions . . . [and] innovations . . . were welcomed. Along with [German artist Albrecht] Dürer, who, like Leonardo, studied [the human body] and proportion, other great Northern [European] masters were seduced by his genius. Among them was the German Hans Holbein . . . whose half-length female figures bore the stamp of Leonardo; the Fleming Quentin Metsys . . . [whose] costume scenes and religious paintings . . . show the likely influence of Leonardo . . . and Joos van Cleve, master painter of the guild of Antwerp. The practical influence of Leonardo was still to be seen in individuals as far removed as [the seventeenth-century painters Peter Paul] Rubens and Rembrandt.

Francesca Debolini. *Artbook: Leonardo da Vinci*. Translated by John Gilbert. New York: Dorling Kindersley, 1999, pp. 130–131.

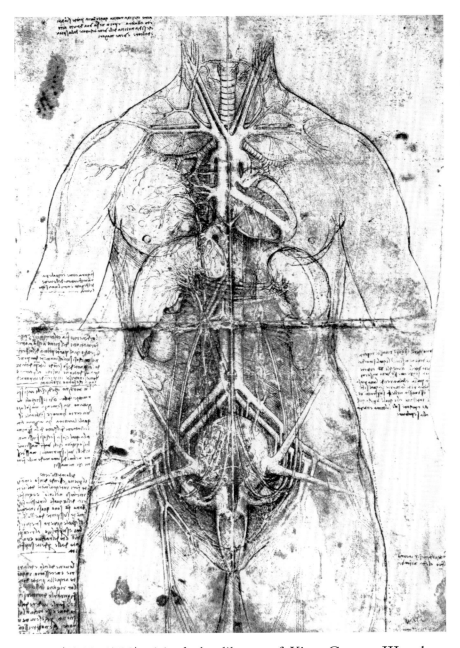

Leonardo has had a profound and ongoing influence on doctors and the science of medicine. He was the first to introduce the practice of creating anatomical drawings, one of which appears here.

(1718–1783) visited the library of King George III, where many of Leonardo's old drawings were then stored. There, Hunter became the first trained scientist to examine them in detail since the artist's death more than two and a half centuries before. In a later lecture about Leonardo, he said that the sketches had allowed him to carry the history of the improvement of anatomy farther back than has been generally done [before] and to introduce into the annals of our art, a genius of the first rate, Leonardo da Vinci, who has been overlooked because he was of another profession and because he published nothing on the subject. I believe he was, by far, the best anatomist . . . of his time, and [he] was certainly the first man we know of who introduced the practice of making anatomical drawings.[71]

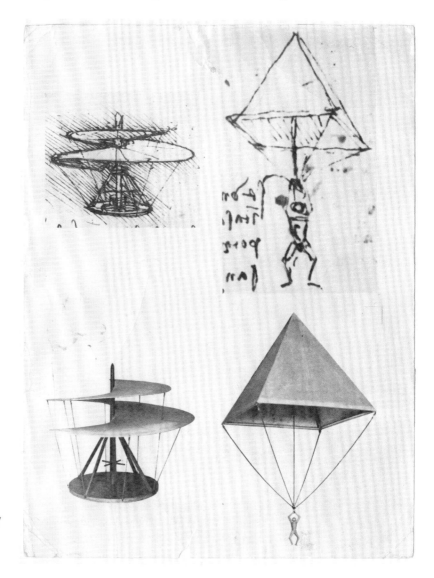

Leonardo's drawings of flying machines inspired Russian American aviation pioneer Igor Sikorsky to invent the first helicopter.

In a similar manner, Leonardo's far-ranging artistic renderings of futuristic gadgets had direct influences on a number of key early modern inventors. One was Igor Sikorsky (1889–1972), the Russian American aviation pioneer who built some of the first modern helicopters. According to the National Aviation Hall of Fame:

> One of Sikorsky's earliest recollections is of his mother telling him of Leonardo da Vinci's attempts to design a flying machine. From that moment on the dream of flight captured his imagination, even though he was repeatedly told that flying had been proven impossible. Finally, at the age of about 12, Sikorsky made a model of a crude helicopter. Powered by rubber bands, the model rose into the air. Now he knew that his dream was not a foolhardy impossibility.[72]

# His Incredible Versatility

Hunter, Sikorsky, and other later scientists who felt Leonardo's influence were specialists in their fields. In contrast, Leonardo himself was a generalist—part painter, part sculptor, part architect, part scientist, and part engineer, a true universal intellect who expressed his many talents directly through his art. The very fact of his incredible versatility frames another important part of his legacy. Namely, he set an example for other far-thinking multitalented people in future ages.

Leonardo was able to excel in so many areas of human knowledge because his mind had a different way of assimilating and analyzing information than the minds of most people. Today, for instance, knowledge is separated into fairly narrow subject areas, sometimes almost rigidly so. "We divide up our knowledge according to disciplines and demand logic from them," Stefan Klein explains. However, Leonardo

> regarded the world as a single entity and sought similarities between the most dissimilar phenomena. We try to solve problems as systematically [precisely and

carefully] as possible. He did so by employing creative combinations. We want answers. He posed questions. But there is nothing to stop us from learning from Leonardo's approach—not to replace the modern way of thinking, but to supplement it. Above all, [he] demonstrated how far a person can take research that has no set goal. Driven by curiosity, he worked for the sheer pleasure of understanding the world.[73]

# A Man of Mystery?

The attention paid in recent times to Leonardo's tremendous versatility has been matched by the image of him as a secretive, even shadowy individual. One factor that has given the general public this impression is his frequent habit of writing his notes backward, as if trying to hide their content. His failure to publish his writings has also been interpreted by some as an attempt to keep secrets. In addition, there is the mysterious smile on the face of the woman he depicted in the *Mona Lisa*. That unique, puzzling grin, along with the fact that the woman remains unidentified, has given many people the impression that the artist purposely kept her anonymous.

Biographers and other scholars who have closely studied Leonardo's life say that none of these factors are reasons for thinking he was intentionally secretive. He wrote in mirror images because he was left-handed, they point out. Also, he did not publish his writings because he was too busy to find the time. Finally, Mona Lisa's identity was almost certainly known to his circle of acquaintances, and he should not be blamed for the confusion that later clouded that information.

Nevertheless, Leonardo's reputation as a mystery man is too well imbedded in the popular consciousness to be banished by the actual evidence. So it has persisted. As a result, all sorts of unfounded theories about him have been proposed and perpetuated over time, especially in the twentieth century.

The most famous example is the still ongoing controversy surrounding Leonardo's supposed involvement in a secret society

*Leonardo's marvelous ability to imagine ideas and machines that would exist in a world far in his future is no better illustrated than in his designs and even his working model for a rudimentary robot. The popular website Leonardo-da-Vinci-Biography.com provides this summary of his ingenious device, which was clearly centuries ahead of its time.*

**L**eonardo created his robot to prove to himself that a human being's body could be imitated. He also built it to showcase it in working mode at parties for his patron Lodovico Sforza. The [robot] would have been the highlight of the party with Leonardo at the helm of the crank powering [it]. . . . Leonardo used his initial studies of anatomy . . . to design the robot. His creation was an extension of his hypothesis that the human body is a machine in structure [and] that its intricate movements could be imitated with the use of engineered machine parts such as levers and pulleys. When Leonardo built his Robot in 1495, it had the capability to walk, stand and sit, open and close its mouth, and raise its arms. . . . [According to Leonardo's drawings] the robot was composed of two working structures. Firstly, there was a four-factor system that controlled the hands, wrists, elbows and shoulders. Secondly, there was a tri-factor system, which controlled the hips, knees and ankles. . . . The lower body . . . was powered by a crank via a cable, which in turn was connected to all the component parts of the leg.

Leonardo da Vinci Biography.com. "Leonardo da Vinci and His Robots." www.leonardo-da-vinci-biography.com/da-vinci-robotic.html.

*A boy in China looks at a model of Leonardo's robot knight. The model was constructed based on the artist's drawings.*

The reputation of Leonardo as a man of mystery was further enhanced with the 2003 publication of the book *The Da Vinci Code* by Dan Brown (pictured). The controversial novel explores Leonardo's alleged involvement in the Priory of Sion, a secretive religious society.

called the Priory of Sion. The dispute began in the 1970s with a low-level French government employee named Pierre Plantard. In various interviews, as well as a 1979 BBC documentary, he claimed that he was both a descendant of medieval French kings and a member of the Priory of Sion. That organization, he said, had existed in secret for many centuries. Its goal was to safeguard the bloodline, or descendants, of Jesus of Nazareth and Mary Magdalene, the woman who traveled with Jesus and his disciples. Jesus and Mary had married and produced children, Plantard explained, and that bloodline later produced some of the French royals and eventually Plantard himself. Moreover, Plantard claimed, the Priory of Sion had had many formidable leaders over the centuries. These individuals were called Grand Masters, and Leonardo da Vinci was one of them.

The next link in the chain connecting Leonardo to the secret Priory of Sion was the 1982 nonfiction book *Holy Blood, Holy Grail*. Its authors, Richard Leigh and Henry Lincoln, elaborated on the story Plantard had told while giving the impression that it might well be true. Later, in 2003, popular novelist Dan Brown published *The Da Vinci Code*. This runaway best seller wove an exciting fictional murder-mystery around the "facts" asserted earlier by Plantard, Leigh, and Lincoln. In Brown's book a man investigating the Priory of Sion finds that Leonardo had left behind clues to the secret about Jesus and Mary Magdalene. Among these clues were shapes of letters and symbols imbedded in code in *The Last Supper* and other paintings, hence the word *code* in the novel's title.

Needless to say, Brown's book raised a ruckus with the Catholic Church, which in his story has long been trying to cover up the "truth" about Jesus and his descendants, and thereby to keep the secret. Critics inside and outside the church have apparently been justified in saying that there is nothing to this story about Jesus's marriage, a secret society, and Leonardo's involvement in it. Reliable independent scholars report that Plantard almost certainly made all of it up. Most of these experts do not fault Brown, since he only took some existing controversial ideas and used them to craft a suspenseful fictional account. As noted biblical scholar Bart Ehrman says, "I'd say to readers that they should enjoy it as a work of fiction and not take its fictional claims as factual claims."[74]

Thus, Leonardo emerges from this controversy the same way he entered it—as a brilliant artist whose mind roamed throughout the massive body of human knowledge. This desire of his to go beyond the limits of painting, sculpture, and other specific disciplines and use his artistic talent to investigate other areas of knowledge made him unique among his peers. This approach allowed him to explore unknown regions of the human imagination and thereby help to shape the world lying centuries in his future. In this way, "Leonardo was far more than an outstanding artist," Klein suggests. "In exploring the world around him, he invented it anew."[75]

# Notes

## Introduction: The Universal Man

1. Robert Payne. *Leonardo*. Garden City, NY: Doubleday, 1978, p. xv.
2. Leonardo da Vinci. *The Notebooks of Leonardo da Vinci*. Translated by Jean Paul Richter. Project Gutenberg. www.gutenberg.org/cache/epub/5000/pg5000.html.
3. Quoted in Payne. *Leonardo*, p. xvii.
4. Giorgio Vasari. *Life of Leonardo da Vinci, Painter and Sculptor of Florence*. Internet Medieval Sourcebook. www.fordham.edu/halsall/source/vasari1.html.
5. Serge Bramly. *Discovering the Life of Leonardo da Vinci*. Translated by Sian Reynolds. New York: HarperCollins, 1991, p. 13.
6. Roy McMullen. *Mona Lisa: The Picture and the Myth*. Boston: Houghton Mifflin, 1975, pp. 1–2.
7. Stefan Klein. *Leonardo's Legacy: How Da Vinci Reimagined the World*. New York: Da Capo, 2011, p. 5.
8. Leonardo da Vinci. *The Notebooks of Leonardo da Vinci*.

## Chapter 1: A Fantastically Fruitful Life

9. Quoted in Bramly. *Discovering the Life of Leonardo da Vinci*, p. 424.
10. Vasari, *Life of Leonardo da Vinci, Painter and Sculptor of Florence*.
11. Robert Wallace. *The World of Leonardo*. New York: Time-Life, 1981, pp. 13–15.
12. Quoted in Jean Paul Richter. *The Literary Works of Leonardo da Vinci*. New York: Phaidon, 1970, pp. 326–327.
13. Martin Clayton and Ron Philo. *Leonardo da Vinci: The Mechanics of Man*. Los Angeles: J. Paul Getty Museum, 2010, p. 9.
14. Leonardo da Vinci. *The Notebooks of Leonardo da Vinci*.
15. Maxine Annabell. "Leonardo's Music." Loadstar's Lair. www.lairweb.org.nz/leonardo/music.html.
16. Quoted in Payne. *Leonardo*, pp. 182–183.
17. Quoted in Sherwin B. Nuland. *Leonardo da Vinci*. New York: Viking, 2000, pp. 165–166.
18. Quoted in Ludwig Goldsheider.

*Leonardo da Vinci.* New York: Phaidon, 1959, p. 39.

19. Quoted in Goldsheider. *Leonardo da Vinci*, p. 39.

## Chapter 2: The Paintings Executed Before 1490

20. Bramly. *Discovering the Life of Leonardo da Vinci*, p. 187.
21. Elke Linda Buchholz et al. *Art: A World History.* New York: Abrams, 2007, pp. 144–146.
22. Maxine Annabell. "Leonardo's *The Baptism of Christ.*" Loadstar's Lair. www.lairweb.org.nz/leonardo/baptism.html.
23. Jack Wasserman. *Leonardo da Vinci.* New York: Abrams, 2003, p. 48.
24. Wasserman. *Leonardo da Vinci*, p. 70.
25. Payne. *Leonardo*, pp. 41–42.
26. Quoted in Goldsheider. *Leonardo da Vinci*, p. 15.
27. Leonardo da Vinci. *The Notebooks of Leonardo da Vinci.*
28. Leonardo da Vinci. *The Notebooks of Leonardo da Vinci.*
29. Wallace. *The World of Leonardo*, p. 35.
30. Wallace. *The World of Leonardo*, p. 35.
31. Leonardo da Vinci. *The Notebooks of Leonardo da Vinci.*

## Chapter 3: The Paintings Produced After 1490

32. Buchholz. *Art*, p. 148.
33. Quoted in Wasserman. *Leonardo da Vinci*, p. 92.
34. Vasari. *Life of Leonardo da Vinci, Painter and Sculptor of Florence.*
35. Maxine Annabell. "Leonardo's *Last Supper.*" Loadstar's Lair. www.lairweb.org.nz/leonardo/supper.html.
36. Buchholz. *Art*, p. 145.
37. Leonardo da Vinci. *The Notebooks of Leonardo da Vinci.*
38. McMullen. *Mona Lisa*, p. 1.
39. Robert Cumming. *Annotated Art.* London: Dorling Kindersley, 1995, p. 27.
40. Vasari. *Life of Leonardo da Vinci, Painter and Sculptor of Florence.*
41. Quoted in Klein. *Leonardo's Legacy*, p. 14.
42. Klein. *Leonardo's Legacy*, pp. 29, 32.
43. Quoted in Nick Pisa. "The Painting Once Sold for £45 Is a Long-Lost Leonardo Worth £120 Million." *Mail Online*, July 4, 2011. www.dailymail.co.uk/news/article-2010309/Leonardo-Da-Vinci-Is-long-lost-120m-Salvator-Mundi-painting-authentic.html.

## Chapter 4: Dabbling in Architecture and Sculpture

44. Quoted in Charles Nicholl. *Leonardo da Vinci: Flights of the Mind.* New York: Viking, 2004, p. 223.
45. Bramly. *Discovering the Life of Leonardo da Vinci*, p. 211.
46. Quoted in Nicholl. *Leonardo da Vinci*, p. 406.
47. Leonardo da Vinci. *The Notebooks of Leonardo da Vinci.*
48. Vasari. *Life of Leonardo da Vinci, Painter and Sculptor of Florence.*

49. Quoted in Nicholl. *Leonardo da Vinci*, p. 80.
50. Maxine Annabell. "Leonardo's Sculpture." Loadstar's Lair. www.lairweb .org.nz/leonardo/sculpture.html.
51. Nicholl. *Leonardo da Vinci*, p. 125.
52. Quoted in Goldsheider. *Leonardo da Vinci*, p. 33.
53. Leonardo da Vinci. *The Notebooks of Leonardo da Vinci*.
54. Quoted in Payne. *Leonardo*, p. 14.
55. Quoted in Ladislao Reti, ed. *The Unknown Leonardo*. New York: Abradale, 1990, pp. 98, 102.

## Chapter 5: Recording Visual Reality: The Drawings

56. Wasserman. *Leonardo da Vinci*, p. 28.
57. Wallace. *The World of Leonardo*, p. 110.
58. Bramly. *Discovering the Life of Leonardo da Vinci*, pp. 19–20.
59. Nicholl. *Leonardo da Vinci*, p. 147.
60. Clayton. "Leonardo in 1510."
61. Clayton and Philo. *Leonardo da Vinci*, p. 124.
62. Maxine Annabell. "Leonardo's Battleships." Loadstar's Lair. www.lairweb .org.nz/leonardo/ships.html

63. Quoted in Reti. *The Unknown Leonardo*, p. 168.
64. Quoted in Reti. *The Unknown Leonardo*, p. 177.
65. Quoted in Reti. *The Unknown Leonardo*, p. 178.
66. Klein. *Leonardo's Legacy*, p. 116.
67. Quoted in Bramly. *Discovering the Life of Leonardo da Vinci*, p. 288.

## Chapter 6: Leonardo's Enduring Legacy

68. Marco Rosci. *Leonardo*. New York: Mayflower, 1981, p. 149.
69. McMullen. *Mona Lisa*, p. 28.
70. Klein. *Leonardo's Legacy*, pp. 3, 7.
71. Quoted in Clayton and Philo. *Leonardo da Vinci*, p. 28.
72. National Aviation Hall of Fame. "Igor Sikorsky: Industrialist, Inventor." http://www.nationalaviation .org/sikorsky-igor.
73. Klein. *Leonardo's Legacy*, p. 222.
74. Quoted in Stone Philips. "Secrets Behind 'The Da Vinci Code.'" *Dateline NBC*. www.msnbc.msn .com/id/7491383/ns/dateline_nbc/ t/secrets-behind-da-vinci-code.
75. Klein. *Leonardo's Legacy*, p. 8.

# For More Information

## Books

Bulent Atalay. *Leonardo's Universe: The Renaissance World of Leonardo da Vinci*. Washington, DC: National Geographic, 2009. A visually splendid, very easy-to-read description of the society in which Leonardo lived and worked and his place and achievements within it.

Wendy Beckett. *The Story of Painting*. New York: Dorling Kindersley, 2000. This beautifully illustrated volume vividly discusses all aspects of Western art in easy-to-understand wording. The large section on Leonardo is very well done.

Kenneth Clark. *Leonardo da Vinci: An Account of His Development as an Artist*. London: Folio Society, 2005. A classic modern account of Leonardo, Clark's book is informative and easy to read, so it will appeal to readers of all ages.

David Franklin, ed. *Leonardo da Vinci, Michelangelo, and the Renaissance in Florence*. New Haven: Yale University Press, 2005. The editor has compiled a collection of useful expert observations of the works of these two great artistic masters.

Stefan Klein. *Leonardo's Legacy: How Da Vinci Reimagined the World*. New York: Da Capo, 2011. The latest major overview of Leonardo, Klein's easy-to-read book is a solid entry in the growing literary genre devoted to this gifted artist.

Andrew Langley. *Eyewitness: Leonardo and His Times*. London: Dorling Kindersley, 2000. Like Dorling Kindersley's other books, this one includes many stunning photos and drawings and an easy-to-read text aimed at young people, although adults interested in Leonardo will enjoy this book, too.

Edward MacCurdy, ed. and trans. *The Notebooks of Leonardo da Vinci*. Old Saybrook, CT: 2002. This is one of the latest and best presentations of Leonardo's many writings, a must for any person seriously interested in the great Renaissance man.

Pietro C. Marani. *Leonardo da Vinci: The Complete Paintings*. New York: Abrams, 2000. If not the best, this is certainly one of the best recent collections of all of Leonardo's paintings. The reproductions are excellent, and there is plenty of interesting commentary by the author.

Sherwin B. Nuland. *Leonardo da Vinci*. New York: Viking, 2000. This is a good general look at Leonardo's life and achievements.

Rosalind Ormiston. *Leonardo da Vinci: His Life and Works in 500 Images*. London: Anness, 2011. Both children and adults will enjoy this impressively mounted collection of colorful images, supported by some lively commentary.

Robert Payne. *Leonardo*. Garden City, NY: Doubleday, 1978. Despite the passage of the years since it was published, this remains one of the best-written and most reliable biographies of Leonardo.

John Phillips. *Leonardo da Vinci: The Genius Who Defined the Renaissance*. Washington, DC: National Geographic, 2008. Aimed at young readers, this recent biography of Leonardo is well written and beautifully illustrated.

Luke Syson. *Leonardo da Vinci: Painter at the Court of Milan*. London: National Gallery, 2011. An excellent study of Leonardo's painting career, including his style, techniques, and the paintings themselves.

Jack Wasserman. *Leonardo da Vinci*. New York: Abrams, 2003. This book is valuable for its excellent text by Wasserman, a distinguished expert on Italian Renaissance art.

## Internet Sources

Maxine Annabell. "Portraits." Loadstar's Lair. www.lairweb.org.nz/leonardo/grotesque.html.

Boston Museum of Science. "Causes of Aerial Perspective." www.mos.org/sln/Leonardo/CausesofAerialPerspective.html.

Boston Museum of Science. "Investigating Aerial Perspective." www.mos.org/sln/Leonardo/InvestigatingAerialP.html.

Loadstar's Lair. "Leonardo's *Last Supper*." www.lairweb.org.nzleonardo/supper.html.

Oracle ThinkQuest. "Why Is the Mona Lisa Smiling?" http://library.thinkquest.org/13681/data/link2.htm

## Websites

**The Drawings of Leonardo da Vinci** (www.drawingsofleonardo.org). A collection of several dozen of Leonardo's most renowned drawings. Click on each to see a larger version.

*Mona Lisa*, **Art History Resources** (http://arthistoryresources.net/leonardo-mona-lisa.html). An art expert discusses Leonardo's most famous painting.

# Index

# Picture Credits

Musee du Louvre, Paris/Alfredo Dagli Orti/The Art Archive/Art Resource, NY, 12

Museo del Bargello Florence/Gianni Dagli Orti/The Art Archive/Art Resource, NY, 66

© National Gallery Collection; By kind permission of the Trustees of the National Gallery, London/Corbis, 25

Preparatory drawing for the Last Supper (sepia ink on linen paper), Vinci, Leonardo da (1452–1519)/Galleria dell' Accademia, Venice, Italy/The Bridgeman Art Library International, 49

Réunion des Musées Nationaux/Art Resource, NY, 32, 54

Scala/Art Resource, NY, 51, 70, 72

Scala/Ministero per I Beni e le Attivita culturali/Art Resource, NY, 37

Scala/White Images/Art Resource, NY, 79

Snark/Art Resource, NY, 96

SSPL/Getty Images, 83

St. Jerome, c.1480–82 (oil and tempera on walnut), Vinci, Leonardo da (1452–1519)/Vatican Museums and Galleries, Vatican City, Italy/The Bridgeman Art Library International, 38

St. John the Baptist, 16th century (oil on canvas), Vinci, Leonardo da (1452–1519) (studio of)/Ashmolean Museum, University of Oxford, UK/The Bridgeman Art Library International, 56

The stomach and intestines, c.1508–09 (pen and ink over black chalk on paper), Vinci, Leonardo da (1452–1519)/The Royal Collection © 2011 Her Majesty Queen Elizabeth II/The Bridgeman Art Library International, 82

Studies of the Proportions of the Face and Eye, 1489–90 (pen & ink over metalpoint on paper), Vinci, Leonardo da (1452–1519)/Biblioteca Nazionale, Turin, Italy/The Bridgeman Art Library International, 41

© Summerfield Press/Corbis, 92

© The Trustees of the British Museum/Art Resource, NY, 81

© Wu Hong/epa/Corbis, 99

Young Christ (terracotta), Vinci, Leonardo da (1452–1519) / Eredi Gallant Collection, Rome, Ital/©Mondadori Electa/The Bridgeman Art Library International, 65

# About the Author

Historian Don Nardo is best known for his books for young people about the ancient and medieval worlds. These include volumes on the arts of ancient cultures, including Mesopotamian arts and literature, Egyptian sculpture and monuments, Greek temples, Roman amphitheaters, medieval castles, and general histories of sculpture, painting, and architecture through the ages. Nardo lives with his wife, Christine, in Massachusetts.